IN ASSOCIATION WITH

SQA

D1549682

HODDER GIBSON
Model Papers
WITH ANSWERS

FREE
audio files to accompany this title can be accessed at
www.hoddergibson.co.uk
• Click on the blue 'Updates and Extras' box.
• Look for the 'SQA Papers Audio Files' heading and click the 'Browse' button beneath.
• You will then find the files listed by language and year.

PLUS: Official SQA 2014 & 2015 Past Papers With Answers

National 5
French

Model Papers, 2014 & 2015 Exams

HODDER
GIBSON
AN HACHETTE UK COMPANY

This book contains the official SQA 2014 and 2015 Exams for National 5 French, with associated SQA approved answers modified from the official marking instructions that accompany the paper.

In addition the book contains model papers, together with answers, plus study skills advice. These papers, some of which may include a limited number of previously published SQA questions, have been specially commissioned by Hodder Gibson, and have been written by experienced senior teachers and examiners in line with the new National 5 syllabus and assessment outlines, Spring 2013. This is not SQA material but has been devised to provide further practice for National 5 examinations in 2014 and beyond.

Hodder Gibson is grateful to the copyright holders, as credited on the final page of the Answer Section, for permission to use their material. Every effort has been made to trace the copyright holders and to obtain their permission for the use of copyright material. Hodder Gibson will be happy to receive information allowing us to rectify any error or omission in future editions.

Hachette UK's policy is to use papers that are natural, renewable and recyclable products and made from wood grown in sustainable forests. The logging and manufacturing processes are expected to conform to the environmental regulations of the country of origin.

Orders: please contact Bookpoint Ltd, 130 Park Drive, Milton Park, Abingdon, Oxon OX14 4SE. Telephone: (44) 01235 827720. Fax: (44) 01235 400454. Lines are open 9.00–5.00, Monday to Saturday, with a 24-hour message answering service. Visit our website at www.hoddereducation.co.uk. Hodder Gibson can be contacted direct on: Tel: 0141 848 1609; Fax: 0141 889 6315; email: hoddergibson@hodder.co.uk

This collection first published in 2015 by
Hodder Gibson, an imprint of Hodder Education,
An Hachette UK Company
2a Christie Street
Paisley PA1 1NB

Typeset by Aptara, Inc.

Printed in the UK

A catalogue record for this title is available from the British Library

ISBN: 978-1-4718-6057-7

3 2 1

2016 2015

Introduction

Study Skills – what you need to know to pass exams!

Pause for thought

Many students might skip quickly through a page like this. After all, we all know how to revise. Do you really though?

Think about this:

"IF YOU ALWAYS DO WHAT YOU ALWAYS DO, YOU WILL ALWAYS GET WHAT YOU HAVE ALWAYS GOT."

Do you like the grades you get? Do you want to do better? If you get full marks in your assessment, then that's great! Change nothing! This section is just to help you get that little bit better than you already are.

There are two main parts to the advice on offer here. The first part highlights fairly obvious things but which are also very important. The second part makes suggestions about revision that you might not have thought about but which WILL help you.

Part 1

DOH! It's so obvious but …

Start revising in good time

Don't leave it until the last minute – this will make you panic.

Make a revision timetable that sets out work time AND play time.

Sleep and eat!

Obvious really, and very helpful. Avoid arguments or stressful things too – even games that wind you up. You need to be fit, awake and focused!

Know your place!

Make sure you know exactly **WHEN and WHERE** your exams are.

Know your enemy!

Make sure you know what to expect in the exam.

How is the paper structured?

How much time is there for each question?

What types of question are involved?

Which topics seem to come up time and time again?

Which topics are your strongest and which are your weakest?

Are all topics compulsory or are there choices?

Learn by DOING!

There is no substitute for past papers and practice papers – they are simply essential! Tackling this collection of papers and answers is exactly the right thing to be doing as your exams approach.

Part 2

People learn in different ways. Some like low light, some bright. Some like early morning, some like evening / night. Some prefer warm, some prefer cold. But everyone uses their BRAIN and the brain works when it is active. Passive learning – sitting gazing at notes – is the most INEFFICIENT way to learn anything. Below you will find tips and ideas for making your revision more effective and maybe even more enjoyable. What follows gets your brain active, and active learning works!

Activity 1 – Stop and review

Step 1

When you have done no more than 5 minutes of revision reading STOP!

Step 2

Write a heading in your own words which sums up the topic you have been revising.

Step 3

Write a summary of what you have revised in no more than two sentences. Don't fool yourself by saying, "I know it, but I cannot put it into words". That just means you don't know it well enough. If you cannot write your summary, revise that section again, knowing that you must write a summary at the end of it. Many of you will have notebooks full of blue/black ink writing. Many of the pages will not be especially attractive or memorable so try to liven them up a bit with colour as you are reviewing and rewriting. **This is a great memory aid, and memory is the most important thing.**

Activity 2 – Use technology!

Why should everything be written down? Have you thought about "mental" maps, diagrams, cartoons and colour to help you learn? And rather than write down notes, why not record your revision material?

What about having a text message revision session with friends? Keep in touch with them to find out how and what they are revising and share ideas and questions.

Why not make a video diary where you tell the camera what you are doing, what you think you have learned and what you still have to do? No one has to see or hear it, but the process of having to organise your thoughts in a formal way to explain something is a very important learning practice.

Be sure to make use of electronic files. You could begin to summarise your class notes. Your typing might be slow, but it will get faster and the typed notes will be easier to read than the scribbles in your class notes. Try to add different fonts and colours to make your work stand out. You can easily Google relevant pictures, cartoons and diagrams which you can copy and paste to make your work more attractive and **MEMORABLE**.

Activity 3 – This is it. Do this and you will know lots!

Step 1

In this task you must be very honest with yourself! Find the SQA syllabus for your subject (www.sqa.org.uk). Look at how it is broken down into main topics called MANDATORY knowledge. That means stuff you MUST know.

Step 2

BEFORE you do ANY revision on this topic, write a list of everything that you already know about the subject. It might be quite a long list but you only need to write it once. It shows you all the information that is already in your long-term memory so you know what parts you do not need to revise!

Step 3

Pick a chapter or section from your book or revision notes. Choose a fairly large section or a whole chapter to get the most out of this activity.

With a buddy, use Skype, Facetime, Twitter or any other communication you have, to play the game "If this is the answer, what is the question?". For example, if you are revising Geography and the answer you provide is "meander", your buddy would have to make up a question like "What is the word that describes a feature of a river where it flows slowly and bends often from side to side?".

Make up 10 "answers" based on the content of the chapter or section you are using. Give this to your buddy to solve while you solve theirs.

Step 4

Construct a wordsearch of at least 10 × 10 squares. You can make it as big as you like but keep it realistic. Work together with a group of friends. Many apps allow you to make wordsearch puzzles online. The words and phrases can go in any direction and phrases can be split. Your puzzle must only contain facts linked to the topic you are revising. Your task is to find 10 bits of information to hide in your puzzle, but you must not repeat information that you used in Step 3. DO NOT show where the words are. Fill up empty squares with random letters. Remember to keep a note of where your answers are hidden but do not show your friends. When you have a complete puzzle, exchange it with a friend to solve each other's puzzle.

Step 5

Now make up 10 questions (not "answers" this time) based on the same chapter used in the previous two tasks. Again, you must find NEW information that you have not yet used. Now it's getting hard to find that new information! Again, give your questions to a friend to answer.

Step 6

As you have been doing the puzzles, your brain has been actively searching for new information. Now write a NEW LIST that contains only the new information you have discovered when doing the puzzles. Your new list is the one to look at repeatedly for short bursts over the next few days. Try to remember more and more of it without looking at it. After a few days, you should be able to add words from your second list to your first list as you increase the information in your long-term memory.

FINALLY! Be inspired...

Make a list of different revision ideas and beside each one write **THINGS I HAVE** tried, **THINGS I WILL** try and **THINGS I MIGHT** try. Don't be scared of trying something new.

And remember – "FAIL TO PREPARE AND PREPARE TO FAIL!"

National 5 French

The course

The National 5 French course aims to enable you to develop the ability to read, listen, talk and write in French, that is to understand and use French, and to apply your knowledge and understanding of the language. The course offers the opportunity to develop detailed language skills in the real-life contexts of society, learning, employability and culture.

How the course is graded

The Course assessment will take the form of a performance and a written exam.

The performance will be a presentation and discussion with your teacher, which will be recorded and marked by your teacher.

This book will help you practise for the written exam you will sit in May.

The exams

Reading and Writing

- exam time: 1 hour 30 minutes
- total marks: 50
- weighting in final grade: 50%

What you have to do

- Read three passages of just under 200 words each, and answer questions about them in English.
- write 120–150 words in French in the form of an email, applying for a job or work placement: there will be six bullet points for you to address.

Listening

- exam time: 25 minutes
- total marks: 20
- weighting in final grade: 20%

What you have to do

- part 1: listen to a presentation in French, and answer questions in English
- part 2: listen to a conversation In French, and answer questions about it in English.

How to improve your mark!

Every year, examiners notice the same kind of mistakes being made, and also they regularly come across some excellent work. They give advice in the three key areas of reading, listening and writing to help students do better. Here are some key points from their advice.

Reading

Make sure that your answers include detail in Reading. Pick out detail from longer chunks of language, rather than focusing on individual words. Read the whole message, then pick out the key points, using the questions as a guide as to where to look. Detailed answers are generally required, so pay particular attention to words like assez, très, trop, vraiment and to negatives. Make sure you get the details of numbers, day, times etc right.

Take care when using dictionaries where a word has more than one meaning. Learn to choose the correct meaning from a list of meanings in a dictionary.

Beware of faux amis: journée means day, not journey, travailler means work, not travel, for instance!

In responding to the questions in the Reading papers, you should be guided by the number of points awarded for each question. You should give as much detail in your answer as you have understood but should not put down everything which is in the original text, as you are wasting time. The question itself usually indicates the amount of information required by stating in bold, e.g. "Mention two of them". Often there are more than two possibilities, but choose the two you are happiest with and stick to them. Don't try to give alternatives, just choose the correct number. Note that there will be a question in one of the reading papers which asks about the overall purpose of the writing. This will always be a "supported" question, such as a box to tick or a true/false choice.

You should re-read your answers to make sure that they make sense and that your English expression is as good as it can be.

Listening

This is the paper that improves most with practice. So use the listening papers in this book several times, to get used to the format of the exam.

Not giving enough detail is still a major reason for candidates losing marks. Many answers are correct as far as they go but were not sufficiently detailed to score marks. The same rules as for Reading apply.

You hear each of the Listening texts three times, so make use of the third listening to check the accuracy and specific details of your answers.

Be sure you are able to give accurate answers through confident knowledge of numbers, common adjectives, weather expressions, prepositions and question words, so that some of the "easier" points of information are not lost through lack of sufficiently accurate details.

In responding to the questions in the Listening papers, you should be guided by the number of points awarded for each question, and by the wording of the question. You should give as much detail in your answer as you have understood but should not write down everything you hear. The question itself usually indicates the amount of information required by stating in bold, e.g. "Mention 2 of them".

Make sure you put a line through any notes you have made.

Writing

This, along with Talking, is where students do best. However, frequently, the language used by candidates tackling Writing dips to a basic level and leads to pieces not being truly developed. Make sure you have some good material prepared and learned, ready to use in the exam.

Also, where learners write pieces that are too lengthy, this certainly does not help their performance. So stick to the 20–30 words per bullet point.

The examiners say many of the pieces are vibrant and refreshing in terms of style and content. At the upper level, the majority of candidates write well, and the range of language used is impressive. So look at the success criteria in the answer section and try to model your Writing on it. This applies particularly to the last two bullet points.

You should ensure that you are careful when you read the information regarding the job you are applying for, and make sure your answer is tailored to fit that. Depending on the job, you may have to alter your strengths or the experience you are claiming.

You should refrain from writing long lists of things such as school subjects (and then repeating the list with a past or future verb tense) as part of your answers.

Use the dictionary to check the accuracy of what you have written (spelling, accents, genders etc.) but not to create new sentences, particularly when dealing with the last two bullet points. You should have everything you need prepared when you come into the exam.

Be aware of the extended criteria to be used in assessing performances in Writing, so that you know what is required in terms of content, accuracy and range and variety of language to achieve the good and very good categories. Ensure that your handwriting is legible (particularly when writing in French) and distinguish clearly between rough notes and what you wish to be considered as final answers. Make sure you score out your notes!

You should bear the following points in mind:

- there are six bullet points to answer: the first four are always the same, the last two vary from year to year
- each of the first four bullet points should have between 20 and 30 words to address it properly
- to get a mark of satisfactory or above, you must address the last two bullet points properly
- you should aim to have at least 15 words for each of these last two points, but do not try to write too much for these
- you will be assessed on how well you have answered the points, and on the accuracy of your language
- for a mark of good or very good, you should have some complex language, such as longer, varied sentences and conjunctions

Good luck!

Remember that the rewards for passing National 5 French are well worth it! Your pass will help you get the future you want for yourself. In the exam, be confident in your own ability. If you're not sure how to answer a question, trust your instincts and just give it a go anyway – keep calm and don't panic! GOOD LUCK!

Model Paper 1

Whilst this Model Paper has been specially commissioned by Hodder Gibson for use as practice for the National 5 exams, the key reference documents remain the SQA Specimen Paper 2013 and the SQA Past Papers 2014 and 2015.

National
Qualifications
MODEL PAPER 1

French
Reading

Duration — 1 hour and 30 minutes

Total marks — 30

SECTION 1 — READING — 30 marks

Read all THREE texts and attempt all questions.

MARKS

READING — 30 marks

Text 1

You find this article about a French family's way of going on holiday.

La famille Casse en vacances!

Nous avons un très grand jardin, que nous aimons tous. Avant, notre famille n'aimait pas partir en vacances parce qu'on avait toujours peur de laisser la maison vide et il n'y avait personne pour arroser le jardin ou les fleurs. Mais un jour, on a lu un article dans un magazine qu'il était possible de faire un échange de maison. On s'est tout de suite renseigné et nous avons trouvé que c'était assez simple de trouver des partenaires sur l'internet qui, eux aussi, cherchaient une maison pendant les vacances. Maintenant on part en vacances chaque année chez des gens, qui eux, viennent chez nous.

C'est idéal pour notre famille. On a tout le confort d'une maison et on est loin des touristes. On fait aussi la connaissance des autres familles qui vivent dans les alentours et donc nos deux enfants ne s'ennuient jamais.

De plus, ces vacances ne sont pas chères car il n'y a qu'un billet d'avion. Il y a aussi quelques euros de frais d'agences à payer, mais c'est tout. Le seul inconvénient est qu'on doit faire le ménage avant de partir!

Questions

(a) Why did the Casse family not like going on holiday? Mention **two** things.   **2**

_____

_____

_____

(b) How did they find out about the possibility of doing a house exchange?   **1**

_____

_____

(c) What did they then discover? Mention **two** things.   **1**

_____

_____

(d) Why is this type of holiday ideal for the Casse family? Mention any **three** things.   **3**

_____

_____

_____

(e) Why is this type of holiday not expensive? Complete the sentence.   **1**

These holidays are not expensive, because you only have to pay for

_____

MARKS | DO NOT WRITE IN THIS MARGIN

Text 1 Questions (continued)

(f)   What do the Casse family think is the only problem?   1

_____

_____

Total marks 10

Text 2

You read an article about Internet shopping in France.

---

15 millions de Français achètent en ligne

La France est le pays européen où les utilisateurs d'Internet adoptent le plus vite le commerce électronique.

Entre janvier et mars 2013, 25 millions de personnes ont fait un achat en ligne. C'est 2,5 millions de personnes de plus qu'en 2012. Pourquoi est-ce que les Français aiment de plus en plus acheter sur Internet?

Alors, d'abord c'est vite fait. En plus, on peut commander toutes sortes de marchandises sans quitter la maison et à n'importe quelle heure de la journée. Les sites de vente de personne à personne, comme par exemple Ebay, connaissent aussi un grand succès. Sur ces sites la plupart des gens sont honnêtes. Mais certains prennent l'argent pour un "objet vendu" et puis n'envoient jamais le produit.

Pour éviter ce problème, le gouvernement et les sites ont signé une Charte de Confiance. Ce document fixe des règles pour les échanges entre personnes sur les sites et protège le consommateur. La Charte a connu beaucoup de succès, et a encouragé surtout les personnes plus âgées à avoir confiance quand elles font leurs achats.

Questions

(a)   Which of the following statements is true, according to the article?   1

French people are not very likely to use the internet for shopping	
French people are less likely to use the internet for shopping than other Europeans	
French people are more likely to use the internet for shopping than other Europeans	

MARKS

Text 2 Questions (continued)

(b) How do recent figures show that French people have taken to Internet shopping? Give **two** details.   2

_____

_____

(c) The article notes an advantage of buying online. What is it?   1

_____

(d) What other advantages are talked about? Mention **two** things.   2

_____

_____

(e) What problem can sometimes arise on the "person-to-person" sales sites? Complete the sentence.   2

Some people take _____ and then _____.

(f) What is the "Charter of Trust" intended to do? Mention **one** thing.   1

_____

(g) In what way has it been successful? Mention **one** thing.   1

_____

Total marks 10

MARKS | DO NOT WRITE IN THIS MARGIN

Text 3

You are given this leaflet, as you are thinking of going to France to improve your French!

MONTPELLIER LANGUES

Apprendre le français en France

Vous voulez apprendre à communiquer rapidement en français? Alors **Montpellier Langues** est l'école idéale pour vous.

Montpellier est réputée pour être la ville la plus jeune de France : un habitant sur cinq est un étudiant venu des 4 coins du monde. Grâce à cette jeunesse, Montpellier est une ville qui bouge!

L'école

Montpellier Langues a été fondé il y a douze ans et se situe dans la zone piétonne, à deux minutes à pied de la mairie. L'école occupe un beau bâtiment historique et toutes nos salles de classe sont très bien équipées et climatisées.

L'hébergement

On vous offre un choix d'hébergement dans des familles d'accueil ou des auberges de jeunesse.

Les cours

Les cours ont lieu tout au long de l'année sauf les jours fériés, et ils commencent toujours le lundi. Ils se font en petits groupes et pendant les cours du matin les étudiants travailleront l'écoute, la lecture et l'écrit. L'après-midi les étudiants auront l'occasion de pratiquer la langue dans des situations réelles, par exemple: appeler la gare SNCF pour se renseigner sur les horaires, acheter des produits frais au marché, prendre rendez-vous chez le médecin etc.

Questions

(a) The leaflet says Montpellier is known as the youngest town in France. What reason is given for this?   1

_____

(b) When was the school founded?   1

_____

(c) Where in Montpellier is the school situated? Mention any **one** thing.   1

_____

MARKS

Text 3 Questions (continued)

(d) What are the classrooms like? Mention **one** thing.   1

_____

(e) What type of accommodation does the school offer? Mention any **one** thing.   1

_____

(f) Complete the sentence.   1

Lessons take place all year except _____.

(g) What will the students work on during the morning lessons? Mention any **two** things.   2

_____

_____

(h) In the afternoons, the students will have the opportunity to practice their French in real life situations. Give any **two** examples.   2

_____

_____

Total marks 10

[END OF READING PAPER]

National Qualifications MODEL PAPER 1

French Writing

Duration — 1 hour and 30 minutes

Total marks — 20

WRITING — 20 marks

Write your answer in the space provided.

You may use a French dictionary.

WRITING — 20 marks

You are preparing an application for the job advertised below and you write an e-mail in French to the company.

> Le grand magasin, "les Galeries Lafayette" à Paris offre des stages en entreprise cet été.
>
> Il nous faut de jeunes gens qui parlent l'anglais et le français au moins, qui sont prêts à travailler et qui savent servir nos clients.
>
> Si vous vous intéressez pour cette offre d'emploi, veuillez comuniquer par e-mail avec vos coordonnées a: info@hausmann.galerieslafayette.com

To help you to write your e-mail, you have been given the following checklist of information to give about yourself and to ask about the job.

You must include all of these points:

- Personal details (name, age, where you live)
- School/college/education experience until now
- Skills/interests you have which make you right for the job
- Related work experience
- Languages spoken
- Reason for wanting to work in France

Use all of the above to help you write the e-mail in French. The e-mail should be approximately 120–150 words. You may use a French dictionary.

ANSWER SPACE

MARKS

ANSWER SPACE (continued)

MARKS | DO NOT WRITE IN THIS MARGIN

ANSWER SPACE (continued)

MARKS

ANSWER SPACE (continued)

Page six

[END OF WRITING PAPER]

National Qualifications
MODEL PAPER 1

French
Listening

Duration — 25 minutes

Total marks — 20

Before listening to each item, study the questions for one minute. Listen to each item three times, with an interval of one minute between playing. You should then try to answer the questions about it before hearing the next item.

You may take notes as you are listening to the French.

You may NOT use a French dictionary.

HODDER GIBSON
LEARN MORE

MARKS | DO NOT WRITE IN THIS MARGIN

Item 1

Pauline tells you about the gap year she took after leaving school.

(a) Why were her parents against her taking a gap year? Mention **two** reasons.

2

_____

_____

(b) Pauline's aunt in Portugal offered to let Pauline stay. On what conditions was she allowed to stay with her aunt? Mention any **one**.

1

_____

(c) Unfortunately, Pauline did not get on with her aunt. What **two** reasons does she give for this?

2

_____

_____

(d) What job did Pauline find in Portugal?

1

_____

(e) What did Pauline gain from her year in Portugal? Mention any **one** thing.

1

_____

_____

(f) What is Pauline's overall impression of the year?   Tick (✓) the correct box.

1

Her experiences with her aunt ruined the year for her	
She realises she was too young to have done such a thing	
She found it challenging but a positive experience	

Total marks   8

MARKS DO NOT WRITE IN THIS MARGIN

Item 2

You hear your French assistant being interviewed about his experiences after he left school.

(a) What did Edouard do after his gap year?   1

_____

_____

(b) What did he do to pay for his trip? Mention **one** thing this involved.   2

_____

_____

(c) He enjoyed this job. Mention **two** reasons he gives for liking the job.   2

_____

_____

(d) He tells us why he did not have problems with his customers. Complete the sentences.   2

The customers were in a good mood because _____.

They weren't stressed because they _____.

(e) He also worked in a youth club. Who exactly was this club for?   1

_____

(f) Mention any **two** activities the young people could do.   2

_____

_____

(g) Why did parents like the club? Mention **one** thing.   1

_____

_____

(h) Why did the young people like the club? Mention **one** thing.   1

_____

_____

Total marks 12

[END OF LISTENING PAPER]

National Qualifications
MODEL PAPER 1

French
Listening Transcript

Duration — 25 minutes (approx)

Item number one

Pauline tells you about the gap year she took after leaving school.

You now have one minute to study the question.

Après le lycée et avant de commencer à faire de longues études à la fac, j'ai décidé de prendre une année sabbatique et de voyager en Europe. Au début mes parents étaient contre parce qu'ils croyaient que j'étais trop jeune et qu'il était trop dangereux pour une jeune fille de voyager seule. Heureusement, ma tante qui vivait au Portugal a dit que je pourrais loger chez elle pendant quelque temps. Mes parents ont donc accepté à condition que je les contacte tous les jours et que j'aide ma tante à faire les tâches ménagères. Malheureusement, je me suis mal entendue avec ma tante. Je devais rentrer à 21 heures tous les soirs et je n'avais pas le droit d'inviter mes copains à la maison. Par conséquent, j'ai décidé de louer un appartement avec mes nouveaux amis. Pour payer le logement j'ai trouvé un petit boulot à la plage où je vendais des glaces. J'ai fini par passer toute l'année au Portugal. D'accord, je n'ai peut-être pas fait le tour de l'Europe mais j'ai eu ma première expérience de la vie sans mes parents et j'ai gagné beaucoup de confiance en moi.

(2 minutes)

Item number two

You hear your French assistant being interviewed about his experiences after he left school.

You now have one minute to study the question.

Qu'est-ce que vous avez fait après avoir fini votre bac, Edouard?

D'abord, j'ai pris une année sabbatique parce que je voulais voyager un peu en Europe et puis après je suis allé étudier les langues à l'université.

Qu'est-ce que vous avez fait pour pouvoir payer ce voyage en Europe?

D'abord j'ai travaillé dans un office de tourisme tout près de chez moi. C'était un travail très varié. Par exemple, je devais trouver un logement pour les gens qui visitaient notre région ou bien faire des réservations pour les excursions.

Vous avez aimé ce travail?

Pour moi, il y avait beaucoup d'avantages dans ce job car j'avais l'occasion de parler d'autres langues avec les touristes, je touchais un bon salaire et je ne m'ennuyais jamais! J'avais toujours beaucoup à faire et les journées passaient très vite.

Vous n'avez pas eu des problemes avec les clients?

Normalement les clients étaient de bonne humeur parce qu'ils étaient en vacances. Ils n'étaient pas stressés car ils ne pensaient pas à leurs problèmes.

C'était le seul travail que vous avez fait?

Non, j'ai travaillé aussi chez Club Jeunesse dans ma ville, c'est pour les jeunes âgés de douze à dix-sept ans. Le club est ouvert le week-end et tous les soirs sauf le lundi.

Qu'est-ce qu'on pouvait faire là?

Bien sûr, nous avons proposé des activités sportives. A part ça, on pouvait faire de la peinture ou jouer d'un instrument de musique. En plus, on avait l'occasion de bavarder avec les copains.

Ce Club, c'est populaire chez vous?

Oui, le club joue un rôle très important dans la ville car il offre aux jeunes la possibilité de se rencontrer en sécurité. En plus, les parents sont contents de nos services parce que les jeunes ne traînent pas dans les rues et il y a toujours des adultes pour surveiller leurs enfants.

Pourquoi est-ce que jeunes aiment ce Club?

A mon avis, les ados aiment bien venir au club parce qu'il y a une très bonne ambiance, et surtout parce qu'on organise des activités pour tout le monde.

(2 minutes)

End of test.

Now look over your answers.

[END OF TRANSCRIPT]

Model Paper 2

Whilst this Model Paper has been specially commissioned by Hodder Gibson for use as practice for the National 5 exams, the key reference documents remain the SQA Specimen Paper 2013 and the SQA Past Papers 2014 and 2015.

National Qualifications
MODEL PAPER 2

French
Reading

Duration — 1 hour and 30 minutes

Total marks — 30

READING — 30 marks

Read all THREE texts and attempt all questions.

MARKS

READING — 30 marks

Text 1

You read this article sent to you by your pen pal in Lille about the town's Christmas market, and a competition linked to it.

Venez découvrir le Marché de Noël de Lille: en plein cœur de l'hiver, Lille étincelle et rayonne de joie de vivre !

Chaque année, La Place Rihour accueille le marché de Noël. L'atmosphère est magique. Il y a de grands sapins illuminés et des chorales qui chantent les chansons de Noël.

Il y a plus de quatre-vingts kiosques où on peut acheter des bijoux en argent, des décorations pour le sapin, des produits en cuir et des jouets en bois. En plus vous pouvez déguster des marrons grillés ou faire du patin à glace.

Nous vous conseillons de vous habiller chaudement car il peut faire très froid.

Et cette année, nous offrons quelquechose de plus! Vous pouvez gagner une compétition pour venir découvrir le marché de Noël de Lille.

Cette compétition est ouverte aux jeunes de quatorze à dix-sept ans. Le prix est un séjour à Lille pour quatre personnes et comprend les frais de voyage, le logement et une visite guidée de la ville en minibus.

Pour gagner il faut répondre à la question suivante.

De quelle couleur est le manteau du Père Noël?

Envoyez votre réponse à l'Hôtel de Ville de Lille.

Questions

(a) Why is the atmosphere at the market described as magical? Mention any **one** thing.

1

_____

(b) What can you buy from the kiosks? Mention any **two** things.

2

_____

_____

(c) What else can you do at the market? Mention any **one** thing.

1

_____

(d) What are you advised to do?

1

_____

_____

MARKS | DO NOT WRITE IN THIS MARGIN

Text 1 Questions (continued)

(e) Complete the following sentence.   1

The competition is open to young people between the ages of

_____

(f) What does the trip include? Mention any **two** things.   2

_____

_____

(g) What question must you answer to win?   1

_____

_____

(h) Where do you have to send your answer?   1

_____

Total marks 10

Text 2

You read an article in which two young French people give their views on reality TV, 'la télé-réalité'

Nadine 21 ans

Moi, j'adore la télé-réalité. Quand j'allume la télé je veux me détendre après une longue journée de travail.

Mon émission préférée est «Secret Story». Au début, les gens qui participent dans ces programmes sont des étrangers mais après quelques jours, ils finissent par faire partie de ma vie. J'en parle tout le temps au boulot avec mes collègues et puis à la fin de la semaine il faut absolument que je vote pour mon favori pour qu'il évite l'éviction.

La télé-réalité offre à tout le monde une chance de réussir dans le monde des médias. Même moi, j'ai déjà fait une demande pour faire partie d'une émission dans laquelle on cherche le plus beau mannequin de la France.

Maurice 28 ans

Je comprends pourquoi la télé-réalité est très populaire. Par contre, je trouve les émissions de réalité inutiles et très dangereuses. Elles donnent de faux espoirs aux participants qui ont souvent des difficultés à retrouver une vie normale.

Je trouve vraiment injuste la facilité avec laquelle ces inconnus deviennent célèbres. Moi, je suis musicien professionnel et j'ai dû travailler dur pour être connu.

En plus, il y a maintenant beaucoup d'acteurs et de chanteurs qui ont du mal à trouver du travail et qui se retrouvent souvent au chômage à cause de ces émissions.

MARKS

Questions

(a) Why does Nadine love reality TV? Mention any **one** thing.   1

_____

(b) What does she find interesting about "Secret Story"? Mention any **one** thing.   1

_____

(c) Nadine says the contestants become part of her life. Complete the boxes.   2

I talk about them all the time to	
At the weekend, I have to	

(d) Nadine has applied to appear in a reality TV programme. What will it involve?   1

_____

_____

(e) What does Maurice find unfair about these programmes?   1

_____

_____

(f) Why does he feel this? Mention **two** things.   2

_____

_____

(g) What does he say is often the result of these programmes? Mention any **one** thing.   1

_____

(h) Which of the following statements best describes their points of view? Choose **one** answer.   1

Nadine and Maurice both enjoy reality TV	
Nadine and Maurice both understand why reality TV is popular	
Nadine and Maurice both intend to take part in a reality TV programme	

Total marks 10

MARKS

Text 3

You want to take a year out to work in France. You see an advert on the internet from a Senegalese family looking for an au pair to help look after their children.

Notre Famille

Nous sommes une famille sénégalaise. Nous habitons depuis douze ans en France. Nous travaillons tous les deux comme médécins, et nous cherchons une jeune personne pour être au pair pour nos deux filles jumelles âgées de douze ans.

Nous préférerions quelqu'un qui parle l'anglais avec nos enfants car nous pensons partir aux Etats-Unis l'an prochain. Nous cherchons quelqu'un qui veut rester chez nous pendant douze mois, jusqu' à la fin juillet.

Nous habitons un grand appartement au centre de Paris, tout près du Louvre. Vous aurez votre propre chambre qui donne sur la rue principale. Votre chambre est à côté de celle des enfants et vous partagerez une salle de bain avec eux.

Le travail

Vous travaillerez tous les jours sauf le mercredi et le dimanche. Normalement, votre travail commencera à 12h.

Vous aiderez les enfants à faire leurs devoirs et vous vous occuperez d'eux le soir si nous sortons.

Vous ferez de petits travaux ménagers comme le repassage ou aider à la préparation des repas.

Pendant vos jours de congé, vous pourrez suivre des cours de français ou aller vous promener dans les quartiers voisins.

Questions

(a) Mention **two** things about the two girls in the family.

2

_____

_____

(b) Why would the family prefer someone who speaks English?

1

_____

_____

(c) What are you told about your living arrangements? Tick (✓) the **two** correct sentences.

2

Your bedroom must be kept clean.	
You will have the main bedroom.	
Your bedroom is next to the children's.	
You will have to share the bathroom.	

MARKS

Text 3 Questions (continued)

(d) When will you have to work?   1

_____

(e) What will you have to do for the children?   2

_____

_____

(f) You are expected to carry out some household tasks. Mention any **one**.   1

_____

(g) What does the family suggest you could do on your days off? Mention any **one** thing.   1

_____

Total marks 10

[END OF READING PAPER]

National Qualifications
MODEL PAPER 2

French Writing

Duration — 1 hour and 30 minutes

Total marks — 20

WRITING — 20 marks

Write your answer in the space provided.

You may use a French dictionary.

MARKS | DO NOT WRITE IN THIS MARGIN

WRITING — 20 marks

You are preparing an application for the job advertised below and you write an e-mail in French to the company.

Colonie de vacances – Ile d'Oléron

Nous cherchons de jeunes gens enthousiastes et pleins d'énergie pour assister comme animateurs dans notre colonie cet été.

Vous devez parler français et anglais.

Pour ce travail, il faut savoir s'entendre bien avec les enfants!

Vous devez organiser des jeux, des activités sportives et de nombreuses autres activités pour un groupe de 7 enfants de 6 à 13 ans.

Contacter: info@ja-vacances.fr

To help you to write your e-mail, you have been given the following checklist of information to give about yourself and to ask about the job.

You must include all of these points:

- Personal details (name, age, where you live)
- School/college/education experience until now
- Skills/interests you have which make you right for the job
- Related work experience
- Which games, sports and activities you could help organise
- Your experience of working with young people

Use all of the above to help you write the e-mail in French. The e-mail should be approximately 120–150 words. You may use a French dictionary.

MARKS DO NOT WRITE IN THIS MARGIN

ANSWER SPACE

MARKS

ANSWER SPACE (continued)

MARKS DO NOT
WRITE IN
THIS
MARGIN

ANSWER SPACE (continued)

ANSWER SPACE (continued)

[END OF WRITING PAPER]

National Qualifications
MODEL PAPER 2

French
Listening

Duration — 25 minutes

Total marks — 20

Before listening to each item, study the questions for one minute. Listen to each item three times, with an interval of one minute between playing. You should then try to answer the questions about it before hearing the next item.

You may take notes as you are listening to the French.

You may NOT use a French dictionary.

HODDER GIBSON
LEARN MORE

MARKS | DO NOT WRITE IN THIS MARGIN

Item 1

Pauline tells you about her exchange visit to England.

(a) How old was Pauline when she went on the school trip?   1

_____

(b) Why did Pauline and Louise get on well? Mention **two** things.   2

_____

_____

(c) What did the French teacher ask her to talk about? Mention **two** things.   1

_____

_____

(d) Pauline compares her school with those in Great Britain. What did she find different in British schools? Mention any **one** thing.   1

_____

(e) How did Pauline spend the evenings with the family after dinner? Mention any **one** thing.   1

_____

(f) What did Pauline decide to do after her trip to England?   1

_____

(g) What did Pauline think after her visit? Tick (✓) the correct box.   1

English schools were not as good as French ones	
Her visit was a success	
French schools were not as good as English ones	

Total marks   8

MARKS | DO NOT WRITE IN THIS MARGIN

Item 2

You listen to your French assistant being interviewed about how school life in Scotland compares with France.

(a) Why does he like the school he is working in? Mention **two** things.   2

_____

_____

(b) He says the pupils are lucky to have this school. Give **two** reasons.   2

_____

_____

(c) Mention any **two** differences he finds between life in French and Scottish schools.   2

_____

_____

(d) What **two** differences does he notice in the school from ones in France?   2

_____

_____

(e) He says he gets on with the pupils, but what does he think about some of them? How does this show itself?   2

_____

_____

(f) Why does he think he couldn't be a teacher? Complete the sentence.   2

I am not going to be a teacher, because I have neither

_____ nor _____ .

Total marks 12

National Qualifications
MODEL PAPER 2

French
Listening Transcript

Duration — 25 minutes (approx)

Item number one

Pauline tells you about her exchange visit to England.

You now have one minute to study the question.

Quand j'avais 16 ans j'ai participé à un échange scolaire avec mon école. Nous avons passé un mois dans le sud de l'Angleterre avec une famille d'accueil. La famille était vraiment gentille et je me suis très bien entendue avec leur fille, Louise. Elle avait le même âge que moi et on avait les mêmes intérêts, surtout la mode. Tous les matins, j'allais à l'école avec Louise. Les cours de français étaient marrants. Le prof m'a demandé de parler en français de ma famille et de ma ville, c'était vraiment très intéressant. J'ai trouvé l'école très différente de mon lycée. En Grande-Bretagne, les profs sont plus compréhensifs et les élèves portent l'uniforme. Je passais les soirées avec ma famille d'accueil et après le dîner, on jouait aux cartes ou on discutait des différences entre la France et l'Angleterre. J'ai vraiment adoré l'Angleterre et après ce séjour j'ai décidé d'étudier les langues étrangères.

(2 minutes)

Item number two

You listen to your French assistant being interviewed about how school life in Scotland compares with France.

You now have one minute to study the question.

Bonjour, Richard. Comment ça va?

Bien, merci, et bonjour à vous.

Voulez-vous me dire comment vous trouvez l'école dans laquelle vous travaillez à présent?

Eh bien, je l'aime bien. Le collège où je travaille est très moderne. Le bâtiment a été construit il y a deux ans seulement. Il est très propre, et très bien situé dans le centre ville.

C'est une bonne école, donc?

Oui, certainement, et je crois que les élèves ont de la chance dans ce collège parce que dans la cantine il y a des écrans plasma, et en plus les facilités pour le sport sont fantastiques.

Et chez vous, les choses sont différentes?

J'ai remarqué quelques différences entre les collèges français et écossais. En Ecosse les journées sont beaucoup plus courtes qu'en France et les élèves écossais ont moins de devoirs, mais bien sur nous avons plus de vacances!

C'est tout ce que vous avez remarqué?

Ah non, par exemple les salles de classes sont super grandes, avec des ordinateurs partout. C'est nouveau pour moi.

Et comment vous trouvez nos élèves?

En général, je m'entends bien avec les élèves mais je trouve que certains sont très timides et ils ont peur de faire une erreur quand ils parlent français.

Alors, vous trouvez votre travail intéressant?

Oui, j'aime mon travail, c'est très varié et puis j'aime bien tous les élèves avec lesquels je travaille. Ce qui est sûr, c'est que je ne vais pas être professeur parce que je n'ai ni la patience ni l'énergie nécessaire!

Alors merci pour l'entretien, et oui, il faut de l'énergie pour être professeur chez nous!

(2 minutes)

End of test.

Now look over your answers.

[END OF TRANSCRIPT]

Model Paper 3

Whilst this Model Paper has been specially commissioned by Hodder Gibson for use as practice for the National 5 exams, the key reference documents remain the SQA Specimen Paper 2013 and the SQA Past Papers 2014 and 2015.

HODDER
GIBSON
LEARN MORE

National Qualifications
MODEL PAPER 3

French
Reading

Duration — 1 hour and 30 minutes

Total marks — 30

READING — 30 marks

Read all THREE texts and attempt all questions.

READING — 30 marks

Text 1

You read a French magazine, in which students are discussing what they think of after-school classes.

Les cours de soutien

Yannis

Oui, on peut profiter des cours de soutien dans mon collège. Un grand avantage c'est qu'il y a la possibilité de faire ses devoirs et des profs restent souvent jusqu'à 18h pour nous aider. Comme ça, quand on rentre à la maison, on est libre toute la soirée.

Ça aide beaucoup car quand on a des difficultés, par exemple en maths, le prof te donne une explication individuelle alors qu'en classe, il explique pour tout le monde! On peut poser toutes les questions qu'on hésite à poser en classe devant les autres élèves, et les profs prennent le temps de tout expliquer cinq ou six fois s'il le faut. Je suis 100% pour!

Cécile

Moi je suis contre les cours de soutien après le collège pour les raisons suivantes: souvent on se moque des élèves qui y vont. Par exemple dans mon collège certaines personnes ne parlent pas aux élèves qui vont aux classes supplémentaires! En plus, la journée scolaire est très chargée et on a besoin de se détendre. Un autre problème c'est que ça peut coûter cher car il faut payer le transport à la maison après les classes.

Questions

(a) According to Yannis, what advantages are there in attending these extra classes? Mention any **two** things.   **2**

_____

_____

_____

(b) What can the teacher do that is different from normal classes?   **1**

_____

_____

(c) Yannis says that asking questions is easier in these after-school classes. Why? Mention **two** things.   **2**

_____

_____

_____

MARKS | DO NOT WRITE IN THIS MARGIN

Text 1 Questions (continued)

(d) Cécile is against after-school classes. Why? Mention **two** things.　2

_____

_____

(e) What other disadvantage does she say there is? Why is this so?　2

_____

_____

(f) Which of the following statements reflects Yannis' and Cécile's views? Tick (✓) the correct box.　1

They agree that after-school classes can be good for some people	
They disagree totally about the classes	
They share some opinions, but disagree on others	

Total marks　10

Text 2

You read an article in a French magazine for parents, discussing how to deal with teenagers!

Quel bazar dans la chambre! Comment vivre avec un adolescent.

A partir de douze ans, un jeune considère sa chambre comme son espace personnel. Donc, les parents doivent prendre l'habitude de frapper avant d'entrer.

Pour les adolescents, il faut leur faire comprendre que la chambre fait partie de la maison. Donc, ils n'ont pas le droit de, par exemple, peindre les murs sans la permission de parents.

On peut insister aussi sur la propreté. Les ados doivent passer l'aspirateur dans la chambre tous les quinze jours et ils doivent mettre leurs vêtements sales dans le panier à linge une fois par semaine.

L'AUTORITÉ—C'EST INDISPENSABLE

Les adolescents ont besoin de règles. Ces règles forment un cadre qui permet aux enfants de grandir en sécurité. Mais, avec tout le stress du collège et la crise d'identité, l'adolescent va tester ce cadre et contester l'autorité beaucoup plus souvent. Il est important que les parents reconnaissent que leur enfant a grandi et qu'il est capable de penser pour lui-même.

Alors parler, discuter, s'arranger, ce sont des choses indispensables. Gronder, exiger, crier à tue-tête, voilà les choses à éviter.

Glossary

bazar - a mess

MARKS | DO NOT WRITE IN THIS MARGIN

Questions

(a) What should parents do when children reach the age of twelve? Why? **2**

_____

_____

(b) If teenagers want to do something to their room what do they have to understand? Mention any **one** thing. **1**

_____

(c) What should parents insist that young people do to keep their room tidy? Mention **two** things. **2**

_____

_____

(d) The article says teenagers also need rules. What reason does it give? Complete the sentence. **1**

The rules give a framework which _____.

(e) Tick (✓) two reasons that lead teenagers to question authority, according to the article. **2**

They are growing up	
They are stressed at school	
They are having an identity crisis	
They are influenced by their peers	

(f) What do parents need to be aware of? Mention **two** things. **2**

_____

_____

Total marks 10

MARKS | DO NOT WRITE IN THIS MARGIN

Text 3

Your teacher gives you a leaflet and asks if you are interested in taking part in the competition mentioned in it.

Vous aimez parler de langues différentes? Vous aimez bien voyager? Alors, participez à notre concours pour gagner un séjour européen pour votre école.

Notre organisation, Eurostras, cherche des groupes de dix étudiants âgés de quatorze à vingt ans pour participer à notre séminaire européen.

Le séminaire aura lieu à Strasbourg dans l'est de la France au mois de mars de l'année prochaine. Les finalistes y passeront trois jours et seront logés dans une auberge de jeunesse.

Pour gagner une place vous devez dessiner une petite affiche et expliquer en français pourquoi votre école devrait participer, et pourquoi vous trouvez que parler une autre langue est important.

Le programme pour les participants

Premier jour

Tous les groupes se présentent en français et rencontrent les autres participants.

Deuxième jour

Chaque groupe va en ville pour vendre les produits traditionnels de son pays. Par exemple de la nourriture, des drapeaux ou des cartes postales.

Troisième jour

Une visite au Parlement, un bâtiment construit en verre, où les groupes discutent de la politique européenne.

A la fin des trois jours, le groupe qui a le mieux travaillé en équipe gagnera un prix de 500 Euros.

Questions

    (a) Complete the following sentence.   **1**

        The Eurostras organisation is looking for students aged between _____

        _____

    (b) When exactly will the seminar take place?   **1**

        _____

    (c) Where in Strasbourg will the finalists stay?   **1**

        _____

    (d) What do you have to do to win a place at the seminar? Mention **three** things.   **3**

        _____

        _____

MARKS

DO NOT
WRITE IN
THIS
MARGIN

(e) What do the groups do on the first day? Mention any **one** thing.   1

_____

(f) Give any **two** examples of traditional products the groups might sell.   1

_____

_____

(g) On the third day there is a visit to the European Parliament. What do the
groups do during the visit?   1

_____

_____

(h) Which group will win the prize?   1

_____

_____

Total marks 10

[END OF READING PAPER]

N5

National
Qualifications
MODEL PAPER 3

French
Writing

Duration — 1 hour and 30 minutes

Total marks — 20

WRITING — 20 marks

Write your answer in the space provided.

You may use a French dictionary.

MARKS

WRITING — 20 marks

You are preparing an application for the job advertised below and you write an e-mail in French to the youth hostel.

Auberge de Jeunesse Jacques Brel

Cherche du fin mai au fin août de jeunes gens enthousiastes et travailleurs pour venir nous assister dans notre reception.

Vous devez parler français et anglais.

Vous devez vous entendre bien avec nos clients, être prêt à travailler dur, et aussi de temps en temps assister dans la cuisine et avec le nettoyage.

Envoyer un e-mail: brussellsbrel@lesaubergesdejeunesse.be.

To help you to write your e-mail, you have been given the following checklist of information to give about yourself and to ask about the job.

You must include all of these points:

- Personal details (name, age, where you live)
- School/college/education experience until now
- Skills/interests you have which make you right for the job
- Related work experience
- How you can contribute to the day-to-day running of the hostel
- Your experience of travelling and visiting other countries

Use all of the above to help you write the e-mail in French. The e-mail should be approximately 120–150 words. You may use a French dictionary.

MARKS

ANSWER SPACE

ANSWER SPACE (continued)

ANSWER SPACE (continued)

MARKS

ANSWER SPACE (continued)

[END OF WRITING PAPER]

National Qualifications MODEL PAPER 3

French Listening

Duration — 25 minutes

Total marks — 20

Before listening to each item, study the questions for one minute. Listen to each item three times, with an interval of one minute between playing. You should then try to answer the questions about it before hearing the next item.

You may take notes as you are listening to the French.

You may NOT use a French dictionary.

MARKS | DO NOT WRITE IN THIS MARGIN

Item 1

While in France you meet Maryse, who comes from Lyon. She tells you about her everyday life.

(a) How far away from Lyon does Maryse live?   **1**

_____

(b) What does Maryse say about her little sister? Mention any **one** thing.   **1**

_____

(c) What is Maryse's mother's job?   **1**

_____

(d) How does Maryse help out in the house? Mention any **one** thing.   **1**

_____

(e) Which job does Maryse do at the weekend to earn some extra money?   **1**

_____

(f) What does she do with the money she earns from her job? Mention any **one** thing.   **1**

_____

(g) Why does Maryse think part-time jobs are useful for young people? Mention any **one** thing.   **1**

_____

(h) What does Maryse mainly talk about? Tick (✓) the correct box.   **1**

Her plans for the future	
Her need for independence	
Her everyday life	

Total marks 8

MARKS | DO NOT WRITE IN THIS MARGIN

Item 2

You hear Louise, a French exchange student, being asked some questions about her family life.

(a) Louise gets on with her mother. Why does she say this?   1

_____

_____

(b) What does she sometimes have arguments about with her parents?   1

_____

_____

(c) What is her father not happy with? Why?   2

_____

_____

(d) What does she have to do to earn her pocket money? Mention **two** things.   2

_____

(e) Tick (✓) the boxes which are correct   2

She is happy with the money she has	
She does not have enough pocket money	
She would like a part-time job	
Her dad thinks she should get a job at the weekends	

(f) What rules are there if she goes out during the week? Mention **two** things.   2

_____

_____

(g) Why is she not frightened about being out at the weekend? Mention **two** things.   2

_____

_____

_____

Total marks 12

[END OF LISTENING PAPER]

National Qualifications
MODEL PAPER 3

French
Listening Transcript

Duration — 25 minutes (approx)

Item number one

While in France you meet Maryse, who comes from Lyon. She tells you about her everyday life.

You now have one minute to study the question.

Bonjour! Je m'appelle Maryse et j'habite à 5 kilomètres de Lyon avec mes parents et ma petite soeur. Je m'entends très bien avec mes parents mais ma petite soeur est très paresseuse et nous nous disputons tout le temps. Ca m'énerve qu'elle travaille moins que moi à la maison. Ma mère est infirmière et travaille tard, donc le soir je mets la table et je prépare le dîner. Elle apprécie cela. Ma mère me donne de l'argent de poche mais je veux gagner un peu plus d'argent parce que je veux aller en Espagne l'année prochaine. Donc, le week-end, je travaille comme serveuse dans un restaurant à Lyon. Ça me permet de mettre de l'argent sur mon compte en banque pour les vacances, d'acheter des vêtements et de sortir avec mes amis. Je trouve les petits boulots très utiles. Ça donne aux jeunes une première expérience du monde du travail. En plus, celà me donne une sorte d'indépendance de mes parents, bien que j'aie déjà beaucoup de liberté.

(2 minutes)

Item number two

You hear Louise, a French exchange student, being asked some questions about her family life.

You now have one minute to study the question.

Alors, Louise. Tu peux me dire comment tu t'entends avec tes parents?

Je m'entends bien avec ma mère; je trouve qu'elle a des opinions et des attitudes très jeunes, très modernes. En général, ça va avec mon père aussi. Mais parfois, il y a des disputes qui sont provoquées par des questions d'argent.

Alors, les relations sont différentes entre toi et ta mère, et toi et ton père?

Ma mère est vraiment compréhensive et elle a beaucoup de confiance en moi. Je voudrais être exactement comme elle quand j'aurai des enfants. Mon père n'est pas tout à fait content si je sors pendant la semaine. Pour lui, les études sont très importantes.

Tu as dit qu'il y avait des disputes au sujet de l'argent. Tu as de l'argent de poche?

Chez moi, si je veux recevoir de l'argent de poche il y a des choses que je dois faire. Par exemple, je dois sortir la poubelle le dimanche et je garde mon petit frère après le collège.

Et ton argent de poche suffit pour toi?

Mais non, mon argent de poche ne me suffit pas. J'aimerais avoir un peu plus d'argent, mais mon père dit que je devrais trouver un travail le week-end.

Tu crois que tes parents te donnent assez de liberté?

Je trouve que mes parents sont compréhensifs. Ils me permettent de sortir très tard si je leur dis où je vais, et avec qui. Si je sors dans la semaine je dois rentrer à dix heures et, bien sûr, je dois finir mes devoirs avant de sortir.

Et le week-end, c'est différent?

Le week-end j'ai un peu plus de liberté. Pourtant, je ne vais pas au centre-ville parce que c'est trop dangereux. Je n'ai pas peur là où je vais après minuit, car je ne suis jamais seule; j'ai toujours mes copines avec moi. Et puis, j'ai mon portable dans ma poche.

Alors, merci, Louise, pour tes réponses.

End of test.

Now look over your answers.

[END OF TRANSCRIPT]

NATIONAL 5

2014

N5

National Qualifications 2014

Mark

X730/75/01

French Reading

WEDNESDAY, 14 MAY

9:00 AM – 10:30 AM

Fill in these boxes and read what is printed below.

Full name of centre

Town

Forename(s)

Surname

Number of seat

Date of birth

Day   Month   Year

Scottish candidate number

Total marks — 30

Attempt ALL questions.

Write your answers clearly, in **English**, in the spaces provided in this booklet.

You may use a French dictionary.

Additional space for answers is provided at the end of this booklet. If you use this space you must clearly identify the question number you are attempting.

Use **blue** or **black** ink.

There is a separate question and answer booklet for Writing. You must complete your answer for Writing in the question and answer booklet for Writing.

Before leaving the examination room you must give both booklets to the Invigilator; if you do not, you may lose all the marks for this paper.

MARKS | DO NOT WRITE IN THIS MARGIN

Total marks — 30

Attempt ALL questions

Text 1

You are surfing the Internet and read this French article about a survey.

Est-ce que les jeunes Français reçoivent moins d'argent de poche qu'il y a cinq ans?

On a parlé avec 500 parents et leurs enfants. Voici les résultats !

Malgré la crise économique les parents continuent à donner de l'argent à leurs enfants. En fait, les jeunes reçoivent dix euros de plus par mois comparé à 2009. D'ailleurs, les parents disent que le montant augmente avec l'âge de l'enfant.

Que font-ils avec cet argent?

Chez les garçons il s'agit souvent des sorties en ville ou d'aller voir leur équipe préférée tandis que les filles ont plus tendance à économiser leur argent.

Pourquoi les parents donnent de l'argent?

Il y a des parents qui donnent de l'argent comme récompense, par exemple pour un bon bulletin scolaire ou pour les tâches ménagères faites à la maison. Ils offrent aussi de l'argent pour les anniversaires.

Finalement, la plupart des parents sont «pour» l'argent de poche car ça aide leurs enfants à gérer leur budget. S'ils le gèrent lorsqu'ils sont jeunes, ce sera plus facile quand ils seront adultes.

Questions

(a) What is the first question of the survey?   1

_____

_____

MARKS | DO NOT WRITE IN THIS MARGIN

Text 1 Questions (continued)

(b) What was the result of the survey? Tick (✓) the correct statement.   1

Parents have stopped giving money.	
Parents give the same amount of money.	
The amount has increased by 10 Euros over the last 5 years.	

(c) Young people do different things with their money.

    (i) According to the survey, what do boys spend their money on? State **two** things.   2

    _____

    _____

    (ii) What do girls do with their money?   1

    _____

    _____

(d) Parents give money to their children at other times. When? State any **three** things.   3

_____

_____

_____

(e) Most parents are in favour of pocket money. Why? State **two** things.   2

_____

_____

[Turn over

MARKS | DO NOT WRITE IN THIS MARGIN

Text 2

You read an article about learning languages.

Les langues ont une très grande importance. Apprendre une langue nous aide à apprécier le mode de vie d'autres pays et l'apprentissage d'une langue aide à mieux connaître sa propre langue.

C'est aussi un grand atout pour sa carrière professionnelle. Beaucoup d'employeurs veulent que leurs employés parlent au moins une langue étrangère.

Julien parle de son expérience.

«Quand j'étais à l'école les langues étrangères ne m'intéressaient pas car j'avais beaucoup de mal à m'exprimer.

Mais heureusement tout ça a bien changé. Après mes études à la fac, j'ai décidé d'apprendre l'anglais. Je n'arrivais pas à trouver du travail dans mon pays et donc on m'a conseillé d'apprendre une deuxième langue pour élargir mes possibilités d'emploi.

Bien sûr j'ai suivi des cours d'anglais mais j'ai aussi commencé à regarder les actualités télévisées en anglais et j'ai même changé le langage sur mon portable. Après quelques mois j'ai trouvé un travail en Angleterre. Depuis les langues sont devenues ma passion.

J'ai quelques conseils pour ceux qui veulent apprendre une langue. Il faut essayer de passer au moins un an dans le pays et de parler dès le début avec les habitants. Et surtout il ne faut pas avoir honte de faire des fautes, c'est tout à fait normal.»

Questions

(a) What do languages help you to do? State any **one** thing.   1

_____

_____

(b) Languages are also an asset in your professional career. Why? Tick (✓) the correct statement.   1

Many employers want their employees to speak at least one language.	
Employers want their employees to work abroad.	
You can get a better job.	

MARKS

Text 2 Questions (continued)

(c) Why was Julien not interested in languages when he was at school? State **one** thing.

1

_____

_____

(d) Why did he decide to learn English? State **two** things.

2

_____

_____

_____

(e) Apart from taking English lessons what else did he do to help improve his level of English? State **two** things.

2

_____

_____

(f) What advice does he have for those who want to learn languages? State any **two** things.

2

_____

_____

(g) What is Julien's overall opinion of learning languages? Tick (✓) the correct statement.

1

Languages should not be taught in school.	
You should only learn a language to get a good job.	
Languages are important in all aspects of life.	

[Turn over

MARKS | DO NOT WRITE IN THIS MARGIN

Text 3

Whilst in France you read an article about "la Fête des lumières" – the festival of lights.

La Fête des lumières de Lyon qui a lieu le 8 décembre est une des manifestations les plus célèbres de la période de Noël en France.

Les origines datent de 1850 quand il y a eu un concours pour créer une nouvelle statue pour la ville.

Pour fêter la nouvelle statue, tous les gens de Lyon ont allumé des bougies à leurs fenêtres, puis ils sont descendus dans la rue pour regarder la ville toute éclairée et partager ce moment avec leurs amis.

Maintenant cette fête attire plus de 4 millions de visiteurs. Ils viennent pour voir les jardins de fleurs illuminés, les feux d'artifices dans la vieille ville et les images projetées sur tous les bâtiments.

Si vous voulez participer à cette fête merveilleuse, il est conseillé de bien réserver une chambre d'hôtel à l'avance et de s'habiller chaudement car il peut faire très froid à Lyon.

Par contre les résidents du centre-ville ne sont pas tous contents du nombre de visiteurs qui viennent pour la fête. Ils se plaignent qu'il n'y a pas de place pour se garer, qu'il est impossible de dormir à cause du bruit et que les gens jettent leurs papiers par terre.

Questions

(a) What is the festival of lights? Complete the sentence.   1

The festival of lights is one of the most _____

events of the Christmas period in France.

(b) The first festival in 1850 was about a new statue. How did everyone in Lyon celebrate? State any **two** things.   2

_____

_____

MARKS

Text 3 Questions (continued)

(c) This festival today attracts more than 4 million visitors. What do they come to see? State **three** things.

3

_____

_____

_____

(d) What advice is there for people going to the festival? State **two** things.

2

_____

_____

(e) Why are some residents not happy about the number of visitors who come to the festival? State any **two** things.

2

_____

_____

[END OF QUESTION PAPER]

MARKS

ADDITIONAL SPACE FOR ANSWERS

ADDITIONAL SPACE FOR ANSWERS

[BLANK PAGE]

DO NOT WRITE ON THIS PAGE

N5

National Qualifications 2014

Mark

X730/75/02

French Writing

WEDNESDAY, 14 MAY

9:00 AM – 10:30 AM

Fill in these boxes and read what is printed below.

Full name of centre

Town

Forename(s)

Surname

Number of seat

Date of birth

Day   Month   Year

Scottish candidate number

Total marks — 20

Write your answer clearly, in **French**, in the space provided in this booklet.

You may use a French dictionary.

Additional space for answers is provided at the end of this booklet.

Use **blue** or **black** ink.

There is a separate question and answer booklet for Reading. You must complete your answers for Reading in the question and answer booklet for Reading.

Before leaving the examination room you must give both booklets to the Invigilator; if you do not, you may lose all the marks for this paper.

MARKS | DO NOT WRITE IN THIS MARGIN

Total marks — 20

You are preparing an application for the job advertised below and you write an e-mail in **French** to the company.

Employeur: La Belle Bourgogne, Visites Guidées

Titre du Poste: Assistant(e) touristique

Nous nécessitons du personnel d'été pour:

- préparer les pique-niques
- accueillir les touristes avant les visites
- nettoyer et ranger les camionnettes et le bureau à la fin de la journée

Essentiels:

- Une connaissance de la langue française
- Une bonne présentation

Renseignements: Pour plus de détails, contactez M Alligant:

e-mail: visites.bellebourgogne@orange.fr
adresse: 25 rue de Constantine
40260 Saulieu
Tél: 08 76 85 44 25
Fax: 08 76 85 44 26

To help you to write your e-mail, you have been given the following checklist.

You must include all of these points:

- Personal details (name, age, where you live)
- School/college/education experience until now
- Skills/interests you have which make you right for the job
- Related work experience
- Any link you may have with a French speaking country
- A request for information about the working hours.

Use all of the above to help you write the e-mail in **French**. The e-mail should be approximately 120–150 words. You may use a French dictionary.

ANSWER SPACE

MARKS | DO NOT WRITE IN THIS MARGIN

[Turn over

ANSWER SPACE (continued)

ANSWER SPACE (continued)

[Turn over

MARKS DO NOT WRITE IN THIS MARGIN

ANSWER SPACE (continued)

Page six

[END OF QUESTION PAPER]

ADDITIONAL SPACE FOR ANSWERS

Page seven

MARKS | DO NOT WRITE IN THIS MARGIN

MARKS | DO NOT WRITE IN THIS MARGIN

ADDITIONAL SPACE FOR ANSWERS

Page eight

N5

National Qualifications 2014

Mark

X730/75/03

French Listening

WEDNESDAY, 14 MAY

10:50 AM – 11:15 AM (approx)

Fill in these boxes and read what is printed below.

Full name of centre

Town

Forename(s)

Surname

Number of seat

Date of birth

Day   Month   Year

Scottish candidate number

Total marks — 20

Attempt ALL questions.

Write your answers clearly, in **English**, in the spaces provided in this booklet. Additional space for answers is provided at the end of this booklet. If you use this space you must clearly identify the question number you are attempting.

Use **blue** or **black** ink.

You will hear two items in French. **Before you hear each item, you will have one minute to study the questions.** You will hear each item three times, with an interval of one minute between playings. You will then have time to answer the questions before hearing the next item.

You may take notes as you are listening to the French, but only in this booklet.

You may NOT use a French dictionary.

You are not allowed to leave the examination room until the end of the test.

Before leaving the examination room you must give this booklet to the Invigilator; if you do not, you may lose all the marks for this paper.

MARKS | DO NOT WRITE IN THIS MARGIN

Total marks — 20

Attempt ALL questions

Item 1

Patricia talks about her part-time job.

(a) Why does Patricia love her job? State any **two** things.   **2**

_____

_____

(b) She has to cycle to work. Why is this? State any **one** thing.   **1**

_____

(c) She talks about what she has to do in the restaurant.

(i) What is her main job?   **1**

_____

(ii) When there are a lot of customers, what else does she have to do? State any **one** thing.   **1**

_____

(d) In her opinion what advantages does this job have? State any **two** things.   **2**

_____

_____

(e) What is Patricia's overall opinion of her part-time job?

Tick (✓) the correct statement.   **1**

She loves it, but she is badly paid.	
She loves it, but would rather meet her friends.	
She loves it, but it can be busy and tiring.	

MARKS | DO NOT WRITE IN THIS MARGIN

Item 2

You then listen to Philippe who asks Sylvie questions about her part-time job.

(a) How often does Sylvie work in the supermarket? Complete the sentence.   **1**

She works there _____ a week.

(b) Why does Sylvie get on well with her colleagues? State any **two** things.   **2**

_____

_____

(c) Sylvie's job has had an impact on her social life.

  (i) What annoyed her when she started this job?   **1**

  _____

  _____

  (ii) Why is the situation better for her now? State **two** things.   **2**

  _____

  _____

(d) How does she still manage to fit in her homework? State any **two** things.   **2**

_____

_____

(e) How will this experience of working help her find a job in the future? State any **two** things.   **2**

_____

_____

_____

(f) What are her plans for next year? State any **two** things.   **2**

_____

_____

[END OF QUESTION PAPER]

MARKS

DO NOT
WRITE IN
THIS
MARGIN

ADDITIONAL SPACE FOR ANSWERS

ADDITIONAL SPACE FOR ANSWERS

MARKS | DO NOT WRITE IN THIS MARGIN

[BLANK PAGE]

DO NOT WRITE ON THIS PAGE

National Qualifications 2014

X730/75/13

**French
Listening Transcript**

WEDNESDAY, 14 MAY

10:50 AM – 11:15 AM (approx)

This paper must not be seen by any candidate.

The material overleaf is provided for use in an emergency only (eg the recording or equipment proving faulty) or where permission has been given in advance by SQA for the material to be read to candidates with additional support needs. The material must be read exactly as printed.

Instructions to reader(s)

For each item, read the English **once**, then read the French **three times**, with an interval of 1 minute between the three readings. On completion of the third reading, pause for the length of time indicated in brackets after the item, to allow the candidates to write their answers.

Where special arrangements have been agreed in advance to allow the reading of the material, those sections marked **(f)** should be read by a female speaker and those marked **(m)** by a male; those sections marked **(t)** should be read by the teacher.

(t)   **Item Number One**

Patricia talks about her part-time job.

You now have one minute to study the questions for Item Number One.

(f)   Moi, je travaille les week-ends dans un restaurant au centre-ville. J'adore mon petit boulot car il y a une bonne ambiance au restaurant, les mêmes clients reviennent régulièrement, et le travail n'est jamais ennuyeux.

Je commence à neuf heures et je termine à trois heures. Je dois aller au travail à vélo, même quand il pleut, parce que j'habite un village assez loin du restaurant et il n'y a pas de transports en commun.

En ce qui concerne mes tâches, mon rôle principal est de servir les boissons. Mais, quand il y a beaucoup de clients je dois aider dans la cuisine et débarrasser les tables. Ces journées sont très chargées et je suis souvent très fatiguée!

A mon avis les avantages de ce travail sont que les clients sont généreux et nous laissent de bons pourboires et en plus, je peux manger gratuitement au restaurant les jours de travail.

Ce travail me plaît tellement qu'un jour j'aimerais avoir mon propre restaurant.

(2 minutes)

(t) **Item Number Two**

You then listen to Philippe who asks Sylvie questions about her part-time job.

You now have one minute to study the questions for Item Number Two.

(m) **Bonjour Sylvie, ça va ?**

(f) Oui, bien merci.

(m) **Comment va ton nouveau boulot au supermarché?**

(f) Bien, c'est assez intéressant et en plus ça me change du travail scolaire. J'y travaille deux soirs par semaine, ce qui me convient.

(m) **Comment est-ce que tu t'entends avec tes collègues?**

(f) Je m'entends bien avec eux. C'est super car il y en a beaucoup qui ont le même âge que moi, donc on a des choses en commun et on aime sortir ensemble.

(m) **Est-ce que ton travail a changé ta vie sociale?**

(f) Oui certainement. Au début ça m'embêtait que mes amis du lycée se retrouvent au café sans moi. Mais tout va mieux maintenant parce qu'on sort tous les vendredis soirs et on fait la fête ensemble.

(m) **Est- ce que tu as assez de temps pour faire tes devoirs?**

(f) Oui bien sûr, mais il faut que je m'organise. Par exemple, je consacre les dimanches à faire mes devoirs et en plus je ne passe pas des heures devant la télévision comme avant.

(m) **Tu crois que ce travail va t'aider à l'avenir?**

(f) Oui, je crois que cette expérience va beaucoup m'aider quand je chercherai un travail plus tard. D'abord j'ai appris comment gérer mon temps. Et puis, j'ai plus de confiance pour parler aux gens que je ne connais pas et je dirais que je suis devenue plus responsable.

(m) **Et quels sont tes projets pour l'année prochaine?**

(f) Je n'en suis pas encore sûre. Soit je chercherai un emploi à plein-temps soit je passerai un an à voyager en Europe.

(m) **Très bien, tu travailles ce soir ?**

(f) Oui, d'ailleurs il faut que je me dépêche, à bientôt.

(2 minutes)

(t) **End of test.**

Now look over your answers.

[END OF TRANSCRIPT]

[BLANK PAGE]

NATIONAL 5

2015

N5

National Qualifications 2015

Mark

X730/75/01

French Reading

FRIDAY, 22 MAY

9:00 AM – 10:30 AM

Fill in these boxes and read what is printed below.

Full name of centre

Town

Forename(s)

Surname

Number of seat

Date of birth

Day	Month	Year	Scottish candidate number

Total marks — 30

Attempt ALL questions.

Write your answers clearly, in **English**, in the spaces provided in this booklet.

You may use a French dictionary.

Additional space for answers is provided at the end of this booklet. If you use this space you must clearly identify the question number you are attempting.

Use **blue** or **black** ink.

There is a separate question and answer booklet for Writing. You must complete your answer for Writing in the question and answer booklet for Writing.

Before leaving the examination room you must give both booklets to the Invigilator; if you do not, you may lose all the marks for this paper.

MARKS | DO NOT WRITE IN THIS MARGIN

Total marks — 30

Attempt ALL questions

Text 1

Your friend shows you an article in a French newspaper.

Les petits boulots : mode d'emploi

Lola est une collégienne de quinze ans. Elle voudrait travailler pour payer ses vêtements et pour mettre de l'argent de côté pour un voyage. Cependant ce n'est pas très facile pour les jeunes de trouver du travail.

«Personne ne veut me donner du travail! J'ai demandé à une copine de ma mère qui tient un magasin et j'ai même appelé le patron d'une grande entreprise! On m'a dit que j'étais trop jeune et ils m'ont conseillé d'attendre deux ou trois ans. Ce n'est pas juste!!»

Lola n'est pas la seule. La loi en France est très stricte. Les jeunes de moins de seize ans ne peuvent travailler que pendant les vacances scolaires et seulement si ces vacances durent quinze jours ou plus. On ne peut pas travailler plus de cinq heures par jour.

Alors, que doit-on faire pour gagner un peu d'argent?

Et bien, il faut profiter de la famille et des voisins! Aider des personnes âgées à faire des tâches ménagères, donner des cours particuliers à des élèves plus jeunes ou encore tondre le gazon. Mais attention – pour pratiquer tous ces petits boulots, il vous faudra une autorisation parentale. Comme la vie est dure!

Questions

(a) Lola would like to find a job. Why? Complete the sentence.   2

   She would like to find a job to pay for her _____

   and put some money away for _____.

(b) Lola talks about her job search. What did she do to find a job? State **two** things.   2

   _____

   _____

MARKS | DO NOT WRITE IN THIS MARGIN

Text 1 Questions (continued)

(c) Employers told her she was too young. What advice did they give her?   **1**

_____

(d) The law in France is very strict for workers under the age of sixteen. What are the rules? State any **two** things.   **2**

_____

_____

(e) The article suggests you can do some work for your family or neighbours. What could you do? State **three** things.   **3**

_____

_____

_____

[Turn over

MARKS | DO NOT WRITE IN THIS MARGIN

Text 2

You read an article which talks about the use of the Internet to support learning.

Internet et les études

L'usage d'Internet est devenu de plus en plus répandu à travers la France et on dit que c'est un outil de travail indispensable de nos jours. Les avantages sont nombreux — les étudiants peuvent faire des recherches et communiquer avec les gens partout dans le monde, tout en apprenant l'informatique.

La plupart des parents parlent aussi des bénéfices de l'Internet pour aider leurs enfants avec leurs devoirs. Par exemple, l'enfant peut essayer de trouver de l'aide par lui-même ou ses parents peuvent se renseigner pour informer l'enfant.

Néanmoins, il y a aussi des aspects négatifs: en passant des heures devant un écran on perd le contact avec la réalité et on lit moins de livres. Certaines personnes sortent de moins en moins car ils préfèrent rester chez eux à discuter avec leurs amis virtuels. Et attention! Il ne faut pas toujours croire à tout ce qu'on lit sur Internet.

Quant aux professeurs . . . oui, ils voient les avantages apportés par l'internet mais plusieurs problèmes se présentent. Par exemple, il n'y a pas assez d'ordinateurs dans les salles de classe, le système d'informatique est souvent en panne et il est parfois difficile d'accéder aux sites intéressants à l'école.

Questions

(a) The Internet has become more and more widespread in France. Which statement supports this? Tick (✓) the correct box.

1

People work more at home on the Internet.	
The Internet is an essential tool at work.	
You can book your travel in advance using the Internet.	

(b) What are the advantages of the Internet for students? State any **two** things.

2

_____

_____

MARKS | DO NOT WRITE IN THIS MARGIN

Text 2 Questions (continued)

(c) Young people often use the Internet to help with their homework. What benefits do parents see in this? State any **one** thing.   **1**

_____

(d) There are some negative aspects of using the Internet.

  (i) What could happen if you spend hours on the computer? State any **one** thing.   **1**

_____

  (ii) People are going out less. Why?   **1**

_____

_____

  (iii) What do you need to be careful of when you are on the Internet?   **1**

_____

_____

(e) Teachers highlight a number of problems. What are they? State any **two** things.   **2**

_____

_____

(f) What is the author's overall opinion about the Internet to support learning? Tick (✓) the correct box.   **1**

The Internet should be forbidden in schools.	
All learning should be done using the Internet.	
The Internet can support learning when and where appropriate.	

[Turn over

MARKS | DO NOT WRITE IN THIS MARGIN

Text 3

You read an article about food waste.

C'est quoi, le gaspillage alimentaire*?

Le gaspillage alimentaire commence dès la production. Les supermarchés veulent vendre seulement de beaux produits, par exemple, des tomates bien rondes ou des pommes parfaites! Ceci oblige les producteurs de fruits et légumes à faire une sélection stricte et par conséquent, les fruits et légumes qui ont le moindre défaut finissent à la poubelle.

Le gaspillage vient aussi de nos habitudes de consommation. Bien souvent, nous achetons plus que ce que nous consommons réellement, et on jette environ 20% des aliments achetés.

Quelles sont les conséquences de ce gaspillage?

D'abord, l'argent utilisé pour produire ces aliments est gâché. Ensuite, il faut traiter tous ces déchets. Finalement, ce recyclage est une activité qui demande beaucoup d'énergie.

Que peut-on faire pour réduire le gaspillage?

Il existe des solutions très simples pour moins gaspiller à la maison: on devrait faire une liste des courses et n'acheter que la quantité de produits nécessaires. N'oubliez pas: on peut toujours congeler ce qui reste au frigo.

*Le gaspillage alimentaire — food waste

Questions

   (a) Complete the following sentence.   1

       Supermarkets only want to sell beautiful produce such as really round

       tomatoes and _____ .

   (b) Supermarket policy affects fruit and vegetable producers.

      (i) What do the producers have to do?   1

         _____

      (ii) What happens because of this?   1

         _____

         _____

MARKS

Text 3 Questions (continued)

(c) In what ways do the habits of consumers contribute to the amount of food waste? State **two** things.

2

_____

_____

(d) Wasting food has consequences. State any **two** examples of this.

2

_____

_____

(e) What can each household do to help? State **three** things.

3

_____

_____

_____

[END OF QUESTION PAPER]

ADDITIONAL SPACE FOR ANSWERS

MARKS | DO NOT WRITE IN THIS MARGIN

ADDITIONAL SPACE FOR ANSWERS

[BLANK PAGE]

DO NOT WRITE ON THIS PAGE

[BLANK PAGE]

DO NOT WRITE ON THIS PAGE

[BLANK PAGE]

DO NOT WRITE ON THIS PAGE

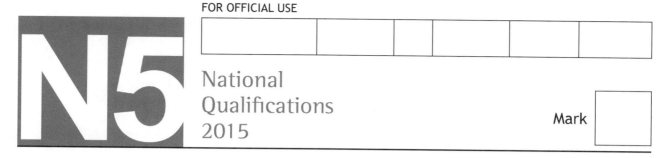

N5

National
Qualifications
2015

Mark

X730/75/02

French Writing

FRIDAY, 22 MAY
9:00 AM – 10:30 AM

Fill in these boxes and read what is printed below.

Full name of centre

Town

Forename(s)

Surname

Number of seat

Date of birth

Day   Month   Year   Scottish candidate number

Total marks — 20

Write your answer clearly, in **French**, in the space provided in this booklet.

You may use a French dictionary.

Additional space for answers is provided at the end of this booklet.

Use **blue** or **black** ink.

There is a separate question and answer booklet for Reading. You must complete your answers for Reading in the question and answer booklet for Reading.

Before leaving the examination room you must give both booklets to the Invigilator; if you do not, you may lose all the marks for this paper.

MARKS | DO NOT WRITE IN THIS MARGIN

Total marks — 20

You are preparing an application for the job advertised below and you write an e-mail in **French** to the company.

Colonie de Vacances
Pour les enfants 5 – 14 ans

Le travail en plein air vous attire?
Vous aimez travailler en équipe?
Vous êtes dynamique?
Vous aimez les enfants?

Le Jardin des Enfants en Normandie

Cherche

animateur/animatrice

Pour les mois de juin à septembre

On vous attend!

To help you to write your e-mail, you have been given the following checklist.

You must include **all** of these points

- Personal details (name, age, where you live)
- School/college/education experience until now
- Skills/interests you have which make you right for the job
- Related work experience
- The reasons why you would like to work with children
- An enquiry about what there is to do in the area on your days off

Use all of the above to help you write the e-mail in **French**. The e-mail should be approximately 120–150 words. You may use a French dictionary.

ANSWER SPACE

MARKS | DO NOT WRITE IN THIS MARGIN

MARKS | DO NOT WRITE IN THIS MARGIN

ANSWER SPACE (continued)

MARKS | DO NOT WRITE IN THIS MARGIN

ANSWER SPACE (continued)

Page five [Turn over

MARKS DO NOT WRITE IN THIS MARGIN

ANSWER SPACE (continued)

[END OF QUESTION PAPER]

ADDITIONAL SPACE FOR ANSWERS

MARKS | DO NOT WRITE IN THIS MARGIN

MARKS | DO NOT WRITE IN THIS MARGIN

ADDITIONAL SPACE FOR ANSWERS

N5

National Qualifications 2015

Mark

X730/75/03

French Listening

FRIDAY, 22 MAY

10:50 AM – 11:15 AM (approx)

Fill in these boxes and read what is printed below.

Full name of centre

Town

Forename(s)

Surname

Number of seat

Date of birth

Day   Month   Year   Scottish candidate number

Total marks — 20

Attempt ALL questions.

You will hear two items in French. **Before you hear each item, you will have one minute to study the questions.** You will hear each item three times, with an interval of one minute between playings. You will then have time to answer the questions before hearing the next item.

You may NOT use a French dictionary.

Write your answers clearly, in **English**, in the spaces provided in this booklet. Additional space for answers is provided at the end of this booklet. If you use this space you must clearly identify the question number you are attempting.

Use **blue** or **black** ink.

You are not allowed to leave the examination room until the end of the test.

Before leaving the examination room you must give this booklet to the Invigilator; if you do not, you may lose all the marks for this paper.

MARKS | DO NOT WRITE IN THIS MARGIN

Total marks — 20

Attempt ALL questions

Item 1

Whilst in France you listen to a young actor who is speaking on a local radio station.

(a) When did the film festival start?   **1**

_____

_____

(b) What will a 30 Euro ticket allow you to do? State any **one** thing.   **1**

_____

(c) You can see the films in their original language. What are the advantages of this? State **two** things.   **2**

_____

_____

(d) After some films you can take part in a debate. What will you have the chance to do there? State any **two** things.   **2**

_____

_____

(e) The actor talks about her film. What is it about? State any **one** thing.   **1**

_____

_____

(f) What is the purpose of the film festival? Tick (✓) the correct box.   **1**

To make money	
To promote international films	
To encourage young people to become actors	

Item 2

Christophe talks to Julie about French cinema and television.

(a) Why is Julie really happy? State any **one** thing.

1

(b) What does Julie love about going to the cinema? Tick (✓) the **two** correct boxes.

2

Eating popcorn and hotdogs	
Watching films on a big screen	
Sharing emotions with friends	
Enjoying the atmosphere	

(c) She says Danny Boon is her favourite French actor. What else does she say about him? State any **one** thing.

1

(d) Why does she not like old French films? State any **two** things.

2

(e) Name any **two** advantages she gives of watching a film at home.

2

(f) What annoys her about French television? State any **two** things.

2

(g) Why does she like watching Channel 5? State **two** things.

2

[END OF QUESTION PAPER]

MARKS

DO NOT
WRITE IN
THIS
MARGIN

ADDITIONAL SPACE FOR ANSWERS

Page four

ADDITIONAL SPACE FOR ANSWERS

Page five

[BLANK PAGE]

DO NOT WRITE ON THIS PAGE

[BLANK PAGE]

DO NOT WRITE ON THIS PAGE

[BLANK PAGE]

DO NOT WRITE ON THIS PAGE

National Qualifications 2015

X730/75/13

French
Listening Transcript

FRIDAY, 22 MAY

10:50 AM – 11:15 AM (approx)

This paper must not be seen by any candidate.

The material overleaf is provided for use in an emergency only (eg the recording or equipment proving faulty) or where permission has been given in advance by SQA for the material to be read to candidates with additional support needs. The material must be read exactly as printed.

Instructions to reader(s)

For each item, read the English **once**, then read the French **three times**, with an interval of 1 minute between the three readings. On completion of the third reading, pause for the length of time indicated in brackets after the item, to allow the candidates to write their answers.

Where special arrangements have been agreed in advance to allow the reading of the material, those sections marked **(f)** should be read by a female speaker and those marked **(m)** by a male; those sections marked **(t)** should be read by the teacher.

(t)   **Item Number One**

Whilst in France you listen to a young actor who is speaking on a local radio station.

You now have one minute to study the questions for Item Number One.

(f)   Bonjour à tous. Je suis là aujourd'hui pour vous parler du festival international des films ainsi que de mon nouveau film.

Le festival a commencé il y a sept ans et chaque année il devient de plus en plus populaire.

Il dure une semaine et il y a beaucoup de films à voir. Vous pouvez acheter un billet pour 30 euros qui vous donne le droit d'aller voir 20 films de votre choix.

Les avantages d'assister au festival sont nombreux. Les films sont en version originale et donc vous pouvez faire la connaissance de différentes cultures et améliorer votre compréhension des langues étrangères.

Après quelques films il y aura la possibilité de participer à un débat. Vous aurez l'occasion de donner votre avis sur le film, rencontrer les acteurs et aussi de vous faire de nouveaux amis.

Cette année vous pourrez voir le film dans lequel j'ai joué. Mon film raconte l'histoire d'une française qui commence une nouvelle carrière en Espagne. Il est à la fois drôle mais aussi émouvant. Je ne vous en dis pas plus, venez le voir. A bientôt.

(2 minutes)

(t)   Item Number Two

Christophe talks to Julie about French cinema and television.

You now have one minute to study the questions for Item Number Two.

(m) Bonjour Julie, comment ça va?

(f) Ça va super bien. C'est le début des vacances et en plus c'est mon anniversaire alors tout va bien.

(m) Génial! tu as des projets pour ce soir ?

(f) Oui, je vais aller au cinéma avec mes copains.

(m) Tu aimes le cinéma ?

(f) Oui, j'adore ça. J'y vais au moins une fois par semaine. Il n'y a rien de mieux que de regarder des films sur un grand écran et de partager ses émotions avec des amis.

(m) Quels genres de film préfères-tu ?

(f) Je n'ai pas de genre préféré mais mon acteur français préféré est Danny Boon. Il me fait vraiment rire et j'aime son accent du nord de la France.

(m) Y-a-t-il des films que tu n'aimes pas ?

(f) Je n'aime pas tellement les vieux films français. Ils sont toujours trop longs, le langage utilisé est très démodé et il y a très peu d'action.

(m) Aimes-tu regarder les films à la maison aussi ?

(f) Je préfère aller au cinéma mais il y a des avantages à regarder les films à la maison aussi. Si on n'aime pas le film on peut changer de chaîne, si on veut aller aux toilettes on peut le pauser et bien sûr c'est gratuit.

(m) Aimes-tu regarder la télé ?

(f) Ça dépend. Ce qui m'énerve à la télé française, c'est qu'il y a des publicités toutes les dix minutes, qu'il y a trop de feuilletons américains et que tous les matins il y a énormément de jeux stupides.

(m) Y-a-t-il quand même quelques bonnes émissions à la télé?

(f) Oui, j'aime regarder la 5. On peut y voir des documentaires très intéressants et ce que j'aime le plus, c'est qu'il y a souvent des émissions en allemand.

(m) Oh c'est bien ça, je devrais la regarder moi aussi. Ecoute, je te souhaite de bonnes vacances et bien sûr un joyeux anniversaire.

(2 minutes)

(t)   End of test.

Now look over your answers.

[END OF TRANSCRIPT]

Page three

[BLANK PAGE]

DO NOT WRITE ON THIS PAGE

NATIONAL 5 | ANSWER SECTION

Reading

Text 1

(a) • Afraid to leave house empty
   • Nobody to water the grass (or flowers)

(b) • Read it in a magazine

(c) • It was easy to find partners on the internet
   • Who were also looking to exchange

(d) • They have all the comforts of a house
   • They are away from tourists
   • They meet people who live locally
   • Their children are never bored
   Any three of the above

(e) • These holidays are not expensive, because you **only have to pay for a plane ticket**

(f) • They have to clean the house before they leave.

Text 2

(a) Which of the following statements is true, according to the article?

French people are not very likely to use the internet for shopping	
French people are less likely to use the internet for shopping than other Europeans	
French people are more likely to use the internet for shopping than other Europeans	✓

(b) • Between **January and March 2013**
   • 25 million people bought something online
   • 2.5 million more than in 2012
   Any two of the above

(c) • It is quick

(d) • You can buy things without leaving the house
   • At any time of day

(e) • Some people **take your money for something** and then **never send it**

(f) • Put in place rules to govern transactions
   • Protect consumers (*either one*)

(g) • Older people particularly now are confident in buying online

Text 3

(a) • One inhabitant in five is a student (from all over the world)

(b) • 12 years ago

(c) • In the pedestrian precinct
   • Five minutes (on foot) from the town hall (*either one*)

(d) • They are well equipped
   • Have air conditioning (*either one*)

(e) • Staying with families
   • In the youth hostel (*either one*)

(f) • Lessons take place all year except **on public holidays**

(g) • Listening
   • Reading
   • Writing
   Any two of the above

(h) • Phone the railway for information
   • Buy fresh produce at the market
   • Book an appointment at the doctor
   Any two of the above

Writing

Candidates will write a piece of extended writing in the modern language by addressing six bullet points. These bullet points will follow on from a job-related scenario. The bullet points will cover the four contexts of society, learning, employability and culture, to allow candidates to use and adapt learned material. The first four bullet points will be the same each year and the last two will change to suit the scenario. Candidates need to address these "unpredictable bullet points" in detail to access the full range of marks.

Category	Mark	Content	Accuracy	Language resource — variety, range, structures
Very good	20	The job advert has been addressed in a full and balanced way. The candidate uses detailed language. The candidate addresses the advert completely and competently, including **information in response to both unpredictable bullet points.** A range of verbs/verb forms, tenses and constructions is used. Overall this comes over as a competent, well-thought-out and serious application for the job.	The candidate handles all aspects of grammar and spelling accurately, although the language may contain one or two minor errors. Where the candidate attempts to use language more appropriate to Higher, a slightly higher number of inaccuracies need not detract from the overall very good impression.	The candidate is comfortable with the first person of the verb and generally uses a different verb in each sentence. Some modal verbs and infinitives may be used. There is good use of adjectives, adverbs and prepositional phrases and, where appropriate, word order. There may be a range of tenses. The candidate uses co-ordinating conjunctions and/or subordinate clauses where appropriate. The language of the e-mail flows well.
Good	16	The job advert has been addressed competently. There is less evidence of detailed language. The candidate uses a reasonable range of verbs/verb forms. Overall, the candidate has produced a genuine, reasonably accurate attempt at applying for the specific job, **even though he/she may not address one of the unpredictable bullet points.**	The candidate handles a range of verbs fairly accurately. There are some errors in spelling, adjective endings and, where relevant, case endings. Use of accents is less secure, where appropriate. Where the candidate is attempting to use more complex vocabulary and structures, these may be less successful, although basic structures are used accurately. There may be one or two examples of inaccurate dictionary use, especially in the unpredictable bullet points.	There may be repetition of verbs. There may be examples of listing, in particular when referring to school/college experience, without further amplification. There may be one or two examples of a co-ordinating conjunction, but most sentences are simple sentences. The candidate keeps to more basic vocabulary, particularly in response to either or both unpredictable bullet points.

Category	Mark	Content	Accuracy	Language resource — variety, range, structures
Satisfactory	12	The job advert has been addressed fairly competently. The candidate makes limited use of detailed language. The language is fairly repetitive and uses a limited range of verbs and fixed phrases, e.g. *I like, I go, I play.* The candidate copes fairly well with areas of personal details, education, skills, interests and work experience but does not deal fully with the two unpredictable bullet points **and indeed may not address either or both of the unpredictable bullet points.** On balance, however, the candidate has produced a satisfactory job application in the specific language.	The verbs are generally correct but may be repetitive. There are quite a few errors in other parts of speech — gender of nouns, cases, singular/plural confusion, for instance. Prepositions may be missing, e.g. *I go the town.* Overall, there is more correct than incorrect.	The candidate copes with the first and third person of a few verbs, where appropriate. A limited range of verbs is used. Sentences are basic and mainly brief. There is minimal use of adjectives, probably mainly after is e.g. *Chemistry is interesting.* The candidate has a weak knowledge of plurals. There may be several spelling errors, e.g. reversal of vowel combinations.
Unsatisfactory	8	The job advert has been addressed in an uneven manner and/or with insufficient use of detailed language. The language is repetitive, e.g. *I like, I go, I play* may feature several times. There may be little difference between Satisfactory and Unsatisfactory. **Either or both of the unpredictable bullet points may not have been addressed.** There may be one sentence which is not intelligible to a sympathetic native speaker.	Ability to form tenses is inconsistent. There are errors in many other parts of speech — gender of nouns, cases, singular/plural confusion, for instance. Several errors are serious, perhaps showing mother tongue interference. The detail in the unpredictable bullet points may be very weak. Overall, there is more incorrect than correct.	The candidate copes mainly only with the personal language required in bullet points 1 and 2. The verbs "is" and "study" may also be used correctly. Sentences are basic. An English word may appear in the writing. There may be an example of serious dictionary misuse.

Category	Mark	Content	Accuracy	Language resource — variety, range, structures
Poor	4	The candidate has had considerable difficulty in addressing the job advert. There is little evidence of the use of detailed language. Three or four sentences may not be understood by a sympathetic native speaker. **Either or both of the unpredictable bullet points may not have been addressed.**	Many of the verbs are incorrect. There are many errors in other parts of speech — personal pronouns, gender of nouns, cases, singular/plural confusion, prepositions, for instance. The language is probably inaccurate throughout the writing.	The candidate cannot cope with more than one or two basic verbs. The candidate displays almost no knowledge of the present tense of verbs. Verbs used more than once may be written differently on each occasion. Sentences are very short. The candidate has a very limited vocabulary. Several English words may appear in the writing. There are examples of serious dictionary misuse.
Very poor	0	The candidate is unable to address the job advert. **The two unpredictable bullet points may not have been addressed.** Very little is intelligible to a sympathetic native speaker.	Virtually nothing is correct.	The candidate may only cope with the verbs to have and to be. Very few words are written correctly in the modern language. English words are used. There may be several examples of mother tongue interference. There may be several examples of serious dictionary misuse.

NATIONAL 5 FRENCH MODEL PAPER 1

Listening

Item 1

(a) • They thought I was too young, and that it was too dangerous for a young girl (to travel alone)

(b) • She contacted her parents every day
• She helped with the housework (*either one*)

(c) • She had to be home by 9 every evening
• She wasn't allowed to bring her friends home

(d) • She sold ice cream on the beach

(e) • She gained a lot of self-confidence

(f) • What is Pauline's overall impression of the year? Tick (✓) the correct box.

Her experiences with her aunt ruined the year for her	
She realises she was too young to have done such a thing	
She found it challenging but a positive experience	✓

Item 2

(a) • He went to university to study languages

(b) • He worked in a tourist office
• He found accommodation for visitors
• He booked excursions (*either one*)

(c) • He got to talk in other languages
• It was well paid
• He was never bored
• There was lots to do
Any two of the above

(d) • He tells us why he did not have problems with his customers. Complete the sentences.
The customers were in a good mood because **they were on holiday**
They weren't stressed because **they weren't thinking about their problems**

(e) • Young people aged 12–17

(f) • Pain
• Play musical instruments
• Chat with their friends
Any two of the above

(g) • Kept their children off the streets
• Meant adult supervision (*either one*)

(h) • A good atmosphere
• Activities were organised for them (*either one*)

NATIONAL 5 FRENCH MODEL PAPER 2

Reading

Text 1

(a) • Illuminated Christmas trees
• Choirs singing Christmas songs
Any one of the above

(b) • What can you buy from the kiosks? Choose **two** things:

Silver jewellery	
Christmas tree decorations	✓
Leather products	
Wooden toys	✓

Any two of the above

(c) • Buy roast chestnuts
• Go skating
Any one of the above

(d) • Wrap up warm

(e) • Complete the following sentence:
The competition is open to young people between the ages of **14** and **17**.

(f) • Travelling costs
• Accommodation
• A tour of the town in a minibus
Any two of the above

(g) • What colour is Santa's coat?

(h) • (Lille) Town Hall

Text 2

(a) • She wants to relax when she gets home from work
• When she switches on the TV (*either one*)

(b) • The people in the programmes are strangers at first
• She gets to know them well after a few days (*either one*)

(c) • Nadine says the contestants become part of her life. Complete the boxes.

I talk about them all the time to	my colleagues at work
At the weekend, I have to	vote for my favourite (so they are not evicted)

(d) • Being a model

(e) • How easy it is to become famous

(f) • He is a professional musician
• He has had to work hard to become well known

(g) • Actors and singers find it hard to get work
• They become unemployed (*either one*)

(h) • Which of the following statements best describes their points of view? Choose **one** answer:

Nadine and Maurice both enjoy reality TV	
Nadine and Maurice both understand why reality TV is popular	✓
Nadine and Maurice both intend to take part in a reality TV programme	

Text 3

(a) • They are twins
    • 12 years old

(b) • They are thinking of moving to the USA next year

(c) • What are you told about your living arrangements? Tick (✓) the two correct sentences.

Your bedroom must be kept clean	
You will have the main bedroom	
Your bedroom is next to the children's	✓
You will have to share the bathroom with the children	✓

(d) • Every day except Wednesday and Sunday
    • From 12 o'clock on (*either one*)

(e) • Help with their homework
    • Look after them in the evenings if the parents go out

(f) • Ironing
    • Helping prepare meals (*either one*)

(g) • Go to French lessons
    • Walk around the neighbourhood (*either one*)

Writing

Please see the assessment criteria for Writing on pages 140 to 142.

NATIONAL 5 FRENCH MODEL PAPER 2

Listening

Item 1

(a) • 16

(b) • She was the same age, and we had the same interests

(c) • Her family and her town

(d) • The teachers are more understanding
    • They wear uniforms (*either one*)

(e) • Playing cards
    • Discussing the differences between France and England (*either one*)

(f) • Study (foreign) languages

(g) • What did Pauline think after her visit? Tick (✓) the correct box.

English schools were not as good as French ones	
Her visit was a success for her	✓
French schools were not as good as English ones	

Item 2

(a) • It's modern
    • It's only two years old
    • It's clean
    • It's in the town centre
    Any two of the above

(b) • In the dinner hall there are plasma screens, and the sports facilities are great

(c) • The days in Scotland are shorter
    • Pupils in Scotland have less homework
    • In France there are more holidays
    Any two of the above

(d) • The classrooms are bigger
    • There are computers everywhere

(e) • They are shy/timid
    • They are frightened to speak French in case they make a mistake

(f) • I neither have the **patience** nor the **energy necessary**

NATIONAL 5 FRENCH
MODEL PAPER 3

Reading

Text 1

(a) • Some teachers stay to help you
   • Your evenings are free when you get home

(b) • You can get an individual answer

(c) • You don't have to ask in front of the rest of the class
   • The teacher can explain things over and over, if you need

(d) • Some people don't talk to pupils who go to the extra classes
   • The school day is very full (and you need to relax)

(e) • It can be expensive
   • If you have to pay for transport home afterwards

(f) • Which of the following statements reflects Yannis' and Cécile's views? Tick (✓) the correct box.

They agree that after-school classes can be good for some people	
They disagree totally about the classes	✓
They share some opinions, but disagree on others	

Text 2

(a) • Knock before going into their children's bedroom
   • The children see it as their private space

(b) • Their room is part of the house
   • They can't paint the walls without permission (*either one*)

(c) • Keep it clean
   • Hoover (once a fortnight)
   • Put their dirty clothes in the washing basket
   Any two of the above

(d) • The rules give a framework which **allows children to grow up safely (in security, feeling secure)**

(e) • Tick (✓) two reasons that lead teenagers to question authority, according to the article.

They are growing up	
They are stressed at school	✓
They are having an identity crisis	✓
They are influenced by their peers	

(f) • Their child has grown up
   • They can think for themselves

Text 3

(a) • The Eurostras organisation is looking for students aged between **14** and **20**

(b) • **Next March**

(c) • In a youth hostel

(d) • Design a poster
   • Explain in French why your school should take part
   • Say why you think speaking another language is important

(e) • Present themselves in French
   • Meet the other participants (*either one*)

(f) • Food
   • Flags
   • Postcards
   Any two of the above

(g) • Discuss European politics

(h) • The one which has worked best as a team

Writing

Please see the assessment criteria for Writing on pages 140 to 142.

NATIONAL 5 FRENCH MODEL PAPER 3

Listening

Item 1

(a) • Five kilometers (three miles)

(b) • She is lazy
• They argue all the time (*either one*)

(c) • She is a nurse

(d) • She sets the table
• Makes the evening meal (*either one*)

(e) • She works as a **waitress** in a **restaurant**

(f) • Saves it for her holidays
• Buys clothes
• Goes out with her friends
Any one of the above

(g) • Give a first experience of work
• Gives her some independence from her parents
(*either one*)

(h) • What does Maryse mainly talk about? Tick (✓) the correct box.

Her plans for the future	
Her need for independence	
Her everyday life	✓

Item 2

(a) • She has **young** or **modern** attitudes or opinions

(b) • (Questions of) money

(c) • Her going out during the week
• He thinks her studies and homework are important

(d) • Take out the rubbish (on Sundays)
• Look after her little brother (after school)

(e) • Tick (✓) the boxes which are correct

She is happy with the money she has	
She does not have enough pocket money	✓
She would like a part-time job	
Her dad thinks she should get a job at the weekends	✓

(f) • She has to be home by ten
• Do her homework before she goes out

(g) • She does not go to the town centre
• She is never alone
• She is with her friends
• She has her mobile phone
Any two of the above

NATIONAL 5 FRENCH 2014

Reading

1. (a) • Do young (French) people/youths/children/ French people receive **less** (pocket) **money** than **5 years ago/2009**?

(b) • The amount has increased by 10 Euros over the last 5 years.
(Third box ticked.)
(NB – More than one box ticked = 0 marks.)

(c) (i) • Going out **in town/city**/going **to town**/going to parties **in town**/outings **to the city**/evenings **in town**.
• (Going to) see/watch/support their **favourite/ preferred/best** team.
(NB – Going out to town to see their team = 1 mark.)

(ii) (Tend to) save their money.

(d) *Any three from:*
• To award their children/as a reward.
• For a **good** school report/doing **well at** school/**good** marks at school/**good** grades.
• For jobs done at home/helping at home/doing household tasks/chores/housework.
• For birthdays.

(e) • It helps children/young people to manage/they (learn to/can) manage their budget/money/ learn about money/can budget.
• It will be easier/easy when they are older/as adults/it helps them as adults/in the future

2. (a) *Any one from:*
• Appreciate (the way of life/lifestyle/form of life in) **another country/other countries**/the way people **in other countries** live/appreciate **other** ways of life.
• Helps us understand our (own) language (better).

(b) • Many employers want their employees to speak at least one language.
First box ticked.
(NB – More than one box ticked = 0 marks.)

(c) • Found it **difficult/hard to/couldn't** express (himself/things)/**was bad at** expression/**wasn't good at/was bad at** expressing (himself/things)/ speaking/talking.
(NB – Tense irrelevant.)

(d) *Any two from:*
• Couldn't find a job **in his country/France** to find a job **in his country**/has never worked **in his country**.
• **Advised** to learn a language/Career Advisor told him to learn a language.
• To **widen/increase/enlarge/have more/other** job possibilities/help his chances of employment.
(NB – Easier to get a job in his own country = 1 mark.)

(e) • Watched **the news/current events/current affairs/ topical issues** (in English).
• Changed the language on his laptop/tablet/ computer/pc/mobile/phone/has the same language on his mobile/etc.

(f) *Any two from:*
  - Spend (at least) **a year** in the country.
  - (From the beginning) speak with the locals/inhabitants/people who live there.
  - Don't be afraid/embarrassed/ashamed to make **mistake(s)**/There is no shame in making **mistake(s)**/There is nothing wrong with making **mistake(s)**/it is normal to make **mistake(s)**.

(g) • Languages are important in all aspects of life. Third box ticked.
  (NB – More than one box ticked = 0 marks.)

3. (a) • Famous/Celebrated

(b) *Any two from:*
  - Put/(lit/light/light up) candles **in the window**.
  - **Went out/Went** (down) into the street(s).
  - **Saw/Watched** the town illuminated/lit up.
  - **Shared** this/the moment with (their) **friends/enjoyed** with **friends/took part** with **friends**.
  (NB – Tense irrelevant.)

(c) • Garden(s)/flowers **illuminated/lit up**/flower garden **light(s)**/garden of flowers **floodlit/floodlight** (accept different spellings of light).
  - Fireworks **in the old town/city**.
  - Pictures/images (projected) onto the building(s)/the building(s) (all lit up) with images/Projections on building(s).

(d) • Book/reserve/(get a hotel/room) in **advance/ahead/early**.
  - Dress warmly/wear warm clothes/jacket/dress appropriately/wrap up warmly (it can be cold in Lyon).

(e) *Any two from:*
  - Nowhere to **park**/hard **to park**/no **parking** places.
  - Can't sleep because of the noise.
  - (People) throwing/dropping paper/trash/rubbish/litter(on the ground/earth/floor).
  (NB – Litter (on its own) = 1 mark.)

Writing

Please see the assessment criteria for Writing on pages 140 to 142.

Listening

Item 1

(a) *Any two from:*
  - Good/nice atmosphere/ambiance.
  - Regular customer(s)/client(s).
  or
  customer(s)/client(s) come(s) back (all the time)
  - Never/not boring.

(b) *Any one from:*
  - Lives (in a village/town) (quite) far away/doesn't live close/near.
  - No/not a lot of (public/other) transport/any specific public transport.

(c) (i) Serving **drink(s)/refreshment(s)/taking drinks orders**.
  (ii) *Any one from:*
    - **Help/aid/assist/work in the kitchen**.
    - Clear/clean/tidy (away) tables.

(d) *Any two from:*
  - The customers are **generous**.
  - Customers leave (good) tips/she gets (good) tips.
  - (she) can eat (for free/at work/at the restaurant/there)/she gets food/to eat/she is allowed her meals (accept any specific meal).

(e) She loves it, but it is busy and tiring.
  (Third box ticked.)
  (NB – More than one box ticked = 0 marks.)

Item 2

(a) Twice/two/2 (evenings/nights/times/days/shifts).

(b) *Any two from:*
  - Same/similar age.
  - (She has/they have) (a lot of) things in common/similar/same interest(s)/she likes/they like the same thing(s).
  - (she likes to/can) **go out** with them/(they like to/can) **go out** together.

(c) (i) **Her friend(s)** met up/used to hang out (at the café)/went (to the café) **without** her/she used to go to a café **with her friend(s)**.
    or
    She didn't have (enough) time **for** (her) friend(s)/couldn't/found it difficult to go out with/hang out with/see/meet/hardly saw her **friend(s)**.

  (ii) - They meet/she goes/hangs out (with them/friends)/ sees them/friends (on/every) **Friday** (evening).
    - They have a party/go partying/go to parties/have a good time/enjoy themselves.

(d) *Any two from:*
  - Organises herself/is (more) organised/organises her time.
  - (does it/homework) on a **Sunday**.
  - Doesn't spend hours/ages/all her/all the time in front of the television.
    or
    Spends less/not as much time in front of the TV (like/as before).

(e) *Any two from:*
  - Has learnt to manage her time.
  - (more) confident (speaking/working) **with people** (she doesn't know)/**the public.**
  - Become **more** responsible/take on **more** responsibility.
(f) *Any two from:*
  - Not sure/doesn't know (yet).
  - Look for/find a (full-time/another/a new) job.
  - (spend a year) **travelling** in/around/to/through **Europe.**

NATIONAL 5 FRENCH 2015

Reading

Text 1

(a) • (her) clothes (any spelling)/garments
  • a trip/a holiday/journey/travelling
  NB – Clothes and holiday interchangeable

(b) • Asked her **mum's friend/a friend of her mum** (who has a shop)
  • Called/phoned/asked/spoke to the (boss) of a (big) company

(c) • To wait/come back/return in two/three years. (Both numbers do not need to be mentioned)/come back in a couple of years/when she is 17/18.

(d) *Any two from:*
  • During the school holidays
  • (Only if) the school holiday lasts two weeks/15 days/14 days (or more).
  • **Cannot/can't/not allowed to** work **more than** five hours **a day/daily/in the daytime OR can only** work five hours **a day/daily/in the daytime** etc.

(e) • Do/help with housework/cleaning/household chores/chores for an **old(er)/elderly** person
  • Give (individual/particular/private) lessons/courses /tutoring to (younger) pupil(s)/student(s)/children/ help younger people with school work/tutor/teach younger people
  • **Mow/cut** the lawn/garden/grass

Text 2

(a) • The Internet is an essential tool at work (Second box ticked)
  (NB – More than one box ticked = 0 marks)

(b) *Any two from:*
  • Do/helps with research/investigations
  • communicate with people/students **from around/ all over/across the world/abroad/everywhere/ anywhere**
  • learn computer skills/learn computing

(c) *Any one from:*
  • The child/the student/the pupil can find help/ information /do it (himself/on his own/instead of asking parents) **OR** they/he/she can find information/help **themselves/himself/on their own**
  • The parent/they can get/give/find **information for/ to inform the child**

(d) (i) *Any one from:*
  • You can lose (any recognisable spelling) contact/touch with reality/real world
  • You read less/fewer books

  (ii) • (Stay at home) to chat/discuss/talk/speak with virtual friends/virtually/on the computer/ internet/online.

  (iii) • Do not **believe** everything (you read/see/ someone says/writes) (on the internet) **OR** Not everything (you read) (on the internet) **is true/ correct.**

(e) *Any two from:*
  • There are not **enough computer(s)** (in each classroom/room/class).

- The computer/system/network/data system/IT (often) does not work/breaks down
- Difficult/hard to **access/reach/get on to/find** (interesting/web/some) sites/some sites are not **accessible.**

(f) • The Internet can support learning when and where appropriate
(Third box ticked)
(NB – More than one box ticked = 0 marks)

Text 3

(a) • **Perfect** apples

(b) (i) • (They have to make/pick/choose) a strict selection (process)/select strictly/strictly select

(ii) • Fruit (and) vegetables/produce with (the slightest) **things wrong/problems/defects/ flaws/with a bit of damage /which are off/not perfect/which aren't up to standard/scratch/ good enough** go in the bin/get thrown away/ wasted.

(c) • Buy more than they eat/need/consume/buy too much food/produce/products
• (In France) **20%** of food is thrown away/wasted/put in the bin
(NB: We buy more than we eat by 20% = 2 marks)

(d) *Any two from:*
• Money used in/on food/fruit and veg **production** is wasted/Money we use **to produce** food/fruit and veg is wasted
• Waste/scrap has to be treated/dealt with/processed /necessary to treat/process waste/recycled
• Recycling uses/requires/needs/demands (a lot of) energy

(e) • (Make/have/use/write) a shopping list/a list of shopping
• (Only) buy/get/purchase the right quantity/ amount/produce/food/stuff needed/necessary/ required. **OR** Don't buy unnecessary/too many products/ more than you need.
• (You can) freeze **leftovers/scraps/food that's left/ the rest/what you don't eat** (in the fridge)

Writing

Please see the assessment criteria for Writing on pages 140 to 142.

Listening

Item 1

(a) • 7 years ago /2008

(b) *Any one from:*
• To see/watch **20** films/up to **20** films
• To see film(s) of your choice/to see film(s) you like/ prefer

(c) *Any one from:*
• (Get to know/appreciate/see/learn about/explore/ understand/experience) different culture(s)/ (it shows/introduces) different culture(s)/ other countries' culture(s)/new culture(s)/(see) differences in other culture(s)
• Improve your (understanding of) (foreign) language(s)/understand language(s)/learn different/ new language(s)/familiarise yourself with other language(s)/great for learning language(s)

(d) *Any two from:*
• Give your opinion about/view on the film/talk about how good the film was
• Meet/interview/question/speak/talk to (the) actor(s)
• Make/meet (new) friend(s)

(e) *Any one from:*
• A (French) woman/man/ person/someone who starts a (new) career/job (in Spain)/finding a (new) career/job (in Spain)
• A (French) woman/man/person/someone who goes to/moves to/is **in Spain**/ lives **in Spain**

(f) • To promote international films
(Second box ticked)
(NB – More than one box ticked = 0 marks)

Item 2

(a) *Any one from:*
• It is the (beginning of)/she is on/going on holiday(s)/vacation
• It is her birthday

(b) • Watching films on big screen
• Sharing emotions
(Second and third boxes ticked)
(NB – 3 boxes ticked maximum 1 mark; 4 boxes ticked = 0 marks)

(c) *Any one from:*
• He makes her laugh/he's (really/truly) funny
• She likes his accent (from the North of France)/She enjoys his accent/She likes the way he speaks/He has a nice/good accent
• He has an accent from the North (of France)/ is from the North (of France)/was born in the North (of France)/lives in the North (of France)

(d) *Any two from:*
• They are **too/very/quite/really** long
• The **language** used is old-fashioned/out of date/not modern/ancient
• Not a lot of/little/no **action**/not much happens/not good **action**/(very) slow/boring

(e) *Any two from:*
• Change the channel/ programme/movie/film/it/ watch something else (if you don't like it)
• **Pause/Stop** it to go to the **toilet/bathroom**
• It is free/no charge/you don't have to pay

(f) *Any two from:*
• (Lots of/too much) **advertising**/(too many/lots of) **advert(s)/commercial(s)** (every 10 minutes/are long) **adverts** every 2 minutes
• (Too many) **American** soap(s)/series/sitcom(s)/ show(s)/programme(s)/it's all **American**/it's like **American** TV/**American** TV show(s) are stupid
• (A lot of) stupid game show(s)/quiz(zes) **OR** game show(s)/quiz(zes) **in the morning OR** stupid programme(s)/thing(s) **in the morning/every morning**

(g) • **Interesting documentaries/documentary** (any recognisable spelling)
• Programmes in **German/from Germany/German** programmes

Acknowledgements

Permission has been sought from all relevant copyright holders and Hodder Gibson is grateful for the use of the following:

Image © dibrova/Shutterstock.com (2014 Reading page 2);
Image © Christopher Oates/Shutterstock.com (2014 Reading page 4);
Image © Pierre-Jean Durieu/Shutterstock.com (2014 Reading page 6);
Image © CREATISTA/Shutterstock.com (2015 Reading page 2);
Image © Pressmaster/Shutterstock.com (2015 Reading page 4);
Image © SasPartout/Shutterstock.com (2015 Reading page 6).

Hodder Gibson would like to thank SQA for use of any past exam questions that may have been used in model papers, whether amended or in original form.